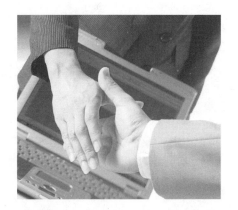

GETTING GRANTS:

THE COMPLETE MANUAL OF PROPOSAL DEVELOPMENT AND ADMINISTRATION

Alexis Carter-Black

Self-Counsel Press Inc.
(a subsidiary of)
International Self-Counsel Press Ltd.
USA   Canada

Printed in Canada.

First edition: 2006; Reprinted 2007
Second edition: 2010

Library and Archives Canada Cataloguing in Publication

Carter-Black, Alexis, 1973-

    Getting grants : the complete manual of proposal development and administration / Alexis Carter-Black. — 2nd ed.

Accompanied by a CD-ROM.

ISBN 978-1-77040-025-2

1. Fund raising — United States. 2. Proposal writing for grants — United States. I. Title.

HG177.C37 2009   658.15'224   C2009-905077-3

Self-Counsel Press Inc.
(a subsidiary of)
International Self-Counsel Press Ltd.

1704 North State Street	1481 Charlotte Road
Bellingham, WA 98225	North Vancouver, BC V7J 1H1
USA	Canada

CONTENTS

TABLE

WORKSHEETS

NOTICE TO READERS

Every effort is made to keep this publication as current as possible. However, the author, the publisher, and the vendor of this book make no representations or warranties regarding the outcome or the use to which the information in this book is put and are not assuming any liability for any claims, losses, or damages arising out of the use of this book. The reader should not rely on the author or the publisher of this book for any professional advice. Please be sure you have the most recent edition.

ACKNOWLEDGMENTS

Oklahoma City Community College (OCCC)

Getting Grants was inspired by my experiences working at Oklahoma City Community College (OCCC). During the more than seven years that I spent at OCCC, I was able to build the Office of Grants and Contracts into a functioning and productive department that provided the faculty and staff of the College with a much needed service. In return, I was given the opportunity to work with a wonderful group of people — including the late Dr. Robert Todd, Dr. Paul Sechrist, Dr. Ann Ackerman, Dr. Max Simmons, Dr. Charlotte Mulvihill, Ms. Patricia Berryhill, and Ms. Barbara Fulton. Thank you all for your support.

Langston University (LU)

As I update *Getting Grants* for this second edition, I want to acknowledge my new work family at Langston University. As I find myself less than six months into my new job as Director of Sponsored Programs, I would like to thank LU's President, Dr. JoAnn Haysbert; the Vice President of Institutional Advancement and Development (IAD) and my boss, Dr. Roderick Smothers; and Mr. Charles King, senior member of the IAD staff. Thank you for providing me with my next great challenge. I am looking forward to making significant contributions to the IAD team and the Langston family.

Thank you to my family:

My husband, Shawn Black, for your love, support, and unwavering belief in me.

My mom, Evelyn Carter, for always supporting me in everything I do and making my life easier.

My children, Breshawn, Ashley, Jacob, and Ainsley, for keeping life interesting!

A special thank-you to:

All my colleagues who shared your experiences with me. You were instrumental to the concept of this book.

Self-Counsel Press and everyone involved in bringing this book to print, including Barbara Kuhne, Senior Editor, for shepherding the book through the process; Audrey McClellan and Tanya Howe for their expert editing; and especially Mr. Richard Day, Acquisitions Editor, for seeing my vision for this book.

INTRODUCTION

I first became aware of grant writing in 1987 while watching my mother write a grant proposal for the nonprofit social service agency in which she worked. In my education and career interests, I have always gravitated toward the social sciences, and government and social service agencies. In later years, these interests expanded to include educational institutions and nonprofit organizations in general. I wanted a career in public service and was strangely attracted to grant writing.

My formal education has allowed me to study political science, sociology, history, public administration, and even regional and city planning. Prior to writing the first edition of this book, my professional experience included providing technical assistance on behalf of an economic development agency; managing donor databases for a university development office; and conducting research and coordinating projects for the state legislature.

At the time that I was writing the first edition of this book, I was working as the Coordinator of Grants and Contracts at Oklahoma City Community College (OCCC), a two-year college without a history of grant writing among its faculty and staff. In this capacity, I was given the opportunity to build a Grants Office where none previously existed. I was later "promoted" to Director of Grants and Contracts. Upon leaving that organization, I spent a brief period of time as Director of Programs at a state government agency, where the primary mission is to grant funds to promote technology-based economic development. I then returned to higher education and currently serve as the Director of Sponsored Programs at a four-year university.

I wrote my first grant proposal in 1996 as a graduate student at the University of Oklahoma. The application was successful, funding a $400,000 renovation of a local nonprofit organization. It is, therefore, not surprising that nine years of my thirteen-year post-college career has been spent directly working in the grants field — writing proposals, running higher education Grants Offices, managing grant-funded projects, and administering funding competitions in the role of grantor. Another nine years during college and early in my professional career, working with grants may not have been the primary function of any positions that I held, but grants were ever-present as a secondary or tertiary responsibility.

I decided to write this book in large part due to my professional experiences at OCCC those first five years. I was the sole employee of the college's Office of Grants and Contracts, responsible for both pre- and post-award activities. I began to notice that colleagues, some within my college and others outside the institution, seemed to think that all they had to do when they were writing and submitting a grant proposal was *write and submit the grant proposal*. I found that many people who had written grants and been awarded funding in the past had little consideration for the process — in other words, what was required of responsible parties before they wrote and submitted a grant proposal, and what responsibilities they had if funding was awarded.

I ran into misunderstanding after misunderstanding about my role in the grants process at the college. Initially I suspected it was just an organizational problem. After all, I was coming to a position that had been vacant for at least a year and a half at an institution that did not view grants as a priority. However, when I spoke with colleagues in similar positions about their experiences at their own organizations, I began to realize a combination of issues contributed to the problem. Not only was there confusion surrounding my role at the college, but I also found that if there were no clear rules about the development and administration of an organization's grant programs, chaos would ensue. If existing rules were not properly communicated to program managers and staff engaged in grant activities, a divide would surely develop between those in administration and those carrying out the daily activities of the organization, many of which were funded by grants.

Obviously, the severity of this disconnect depended on the size of the organization.

Because of the generally larger size and complex organizational structure of most K-12 school districts, colleges, and universities, a carefully crafted grants process is crucial. Such an institution must have a cohesive working process in place to identify need, create programs, develop proposals, and administer grant funds. This is what my college lacked, and a large part of my work at OCCC involved creating rules of grantsmanship, developing the campus's centralized grants office, building a culture of openness in which faculty and staff communicated with the grants office, and discouraging entrepreneurial grant seeking by lone employees of the college. For those organizations that do not have a history with grants, nor a culture of grantsmanship, creating this atmosphere can be a long and difficult process.

My focus in this book is geared more toward educational institutions due to my personal experience working at institutions of higher education. I do, however, have quite a bit of experience collaborating with K-12 school districts and nonprofit organizations and have a broad knowledge about and understanding of the culture of these organizations as well. It is important to note that my emphasis on developing a grants process is applicable to *any* and *all* organizations, large and small, that apply for and receive grant funding. The primary audience for my book is those professionals who work at organizations that have traditionally used grants to support and enhance their programs and operations. Among these are employees of the nonprofit sector; K-12 schoolteachers; college and university faculty; employees of faith-based organizations, research and teaching hospitals, state and local government agencies; and the countless administrators and staff of these and other organizations, who either engage in grant writing themselves or provide technical assistance and administrative oversight to those who do.

In addition to the professional experiences that have led me to write this book, I have had a number of encounters with individuals outside my workplace who have requested assistance with grant writing. I regularly receive telephone and email inquiries; I am approached by acquaintances or by strangers referred to me by people who know what I do for a living. All are looking for grant money (or a grant writer to help them get grant money) in order to start a business, develop technology, pay for school, buy a house, buy a car, etc. Or, they are individuals involved with churches or nonprofit groups that are seeking grant money to fund their various programs. There is a desire in the general population to learn about grants. What are grants? Who can get them? What can you get them for? Where do you get them? How do you get them?

I have seen the wide assortment of infomercials, books, and websites advertising "free government grants" for all sorts of purposes, from starting your own business to buying a house or paying your medical bills. Many of the people who see these ads don't know anything about grants. They buy books, manuals, CDs, and other resources, all in an effort to get the "free" government grants that they are convinced are being given away by the truckload. Often they could easily obtain, at no charge, the information they pay for. These advertisements are misleading, and in my opinion they border on unethical. They are prevalent, and I want to set the record straight about what kind of government grants are

available, what they can be used for, and how they can be accessed.

This book is designed to be a step-by-step guide to grant seeking and will serve as *the* comprehensive manual on the subject of grantsmanship. There are two key lessons that I want everyone to come away with:

1. *Preparation goes a long way in securing grant funding.* Preparation involves an organized system of proposal planning and development, including careful research of the funding source; gaining the support of management to develop and submit the proposal; establishing a reasonable timeline for writing the proposal; creating a reasonable, rational, fundable proposal; being strategic when applying for grant funds; and following up diligently to ensure compliance with funder guidelines.

2. *Accountability starts the day you decide to apply for funding, not the day the funder cuts you a check.* Grant writers must be accountable to their own organizations and respect internal policies and procedures for developing and submitting grant proposals. Organizations must develop and nurture relationships with grant partner organizations. Communication of, and respect for, one another's wishes, needs, and capabilities is essential. Lastly, organizations are accountable to their funding source and must ensure compliance with the rules and regulations of the funder regarding the goals and objectives of funded programs and expenditures of grant funds.

Finally, throughout this book I will stress the idea of *the process*. Grant writing is, indeed, a process — the bulk of which is *not* in the writing.

The first stage in the process is assessing your organization's capacity to pursue grant funds. Every organization must assess its vision, mission, goals, and organizational needs and structure to evaluate whether or not to pursue grant funding and how to go about doing so.

The second stage is identifying and researching funding sources. Finding the right fit between your project and the funding source is crucial to achieving success.

The third stage is developing your proposal. You must ensure that your organization has a solid, well-developed project that meets the needs of its constituency, but which also complements the preferences of the funder.

The fourth stage is writing the proposal, which includes a series of revisions and refinements tailored to the specifications of the grant-making organization.

The fifth stage of the process is the budget phase. When you create the budget for your proposal, it must be aligned with the guidelines of the funding source (which makes your research all the more important), as well as with the written sections of the proposal that detail the project.

Successful proposals are the result of organization, careful planning, and good time management to meet deadlines. And if you win the grant, the process continues, including the phases of project implementation, administration, reporting, and finally grant closeout.

Over the years I have acquired knowledge about grant writing from a variety of sources. Now I would like to share that knowledge. I have designed this book to serve not only as a tutorial on grant writing for first-timers, but also as a comprehensive reference guide that experienced professionals can use to enhance their existing knowledge of grants and improve their organization's processes. If you follow my suggestions, your experiences with writing and submitting grant proposals will be better organized, less stressful, and more pleasant. And if your proposal is funded, knowing what is expected of your organization makes for amicable relationships with funding agencies and grant partners. Good luck with your grant applications!

1

THEY JUST DON'T GET IT, DO THEY?
ASSESSING ORGANIZATIONAL CAPACITY TO PURSUE GRANT FUNDS

I was employed in the business of writing grants — or, more specifically, developing and administering grants — for over seven years as the sole employee in the grants office of an urban community college, the fifth largest in the state. I coordinated the grant-writing activities of more than 750 full- and part-time faculty and staff serving more than 28,000 students and other individuals each year. I'd already had public-sector work experience, which included working with grant programs and writing grants from time to time. I found grants work interesting, and I enjoyed it.

When I accepted the position in 2000, I thought to myself, "I like to write. I like to organize and coordinate. I am a good administrator and have an eye for detail. Working with grants will be the perfect job for me! I'll be able to help the college's faculty and staff find and secure funding for their programs, which in turn will help students. It shouldn't be very stressful. I'll be doing rewarding work. And I can do it … after all, it isn't rocket science!"

Today, I still don't feel that grant writing is rocket science, though that's not to say I think it's easy. However, since entering the grants field in 2000, I have been struck by how the profession is viewed by people on the outside — whether they have little knowledge of the field or have had some experience, even if it's transient, many hold similar ideas about the process of proposal preparation and development.

As I met with colleagues from other colleges, we agreed that "they just don't get it, do they?" We compared notes on faculty who insisted on applying to organizations such as the National Science Foundation for highly competitive and complex grants, basing their proposals on last-minute, ill-conceived ideas and focusing on the number of dollars they could get instead of the real need for a program to exist at their institution. When I was approached by the board of directors of a statewide professional association about how I could provide technical assistance for the association's grant-writing members, I found myself at a loss for words when one of the directors of a member agency declared, "You can't help us. We just lock ourselves away for three days before the grant is due. That's the only way to do it. Just lock yourself away!" They just don't get it, do they?

Two camps emerge: Those who feel that grants are hard work with hard-to-understand rules — hard to write, hard to get funded, and, once funded, hard to administer — and those who think that writing a grant is easy — people get tons of money for all kinds of reasons, the government and foundations are giving away free grant money all the time, and it only takes a matter of days or (worse still) hours to throw together a grant application. The first camp is composed primarily of people who have minimal knowledge of grant activity; they may believe that dealing with grants is more trouble than it is worth, and they generally tend to shy away from grant writing. Members of the second camp are more likely to have worked in or near grant programs in the past. They think that their poorly thought-out, hastily thrown together proposal will succeed in obtaining funding, and they will apply for any source of funding that comes down the pike, based on their belief that they have a "really neat idea that deserves funding."

In reality, grantsmanship is both a science and an art. It is hard work, but gets easier with practice, good planning, and organization. When you need funds for your organization or project, a funded proposal is rarely more trouble than it's worth. Grant proposals often start out as "really neat ideas," but successful proposals are neat ideas that became well-developed, rational plans that matched the needs of the organization seeking funding with the requirements of the funding source.

Is it just people on the outside — people who don't write grants, administer grant-funded programs, or work with grants — who don't get it, or do insiders have some problems as well? In my experience there is enough "blame" to spread around. From novices to seasoned professionals, we all have room to expand our knowledge of the grants landscape. We can all adjust our thinking about grants; our perceptions and misperceptions; and our views about the place of grants in our organizations, the relationship between grant funding and the organization's mission, and the way in which we approach the grants process — before submission and after award.

I want everybody who is engaged in the process of proposal development and administration to "get it." People who get it don't write grants just because the money is available; they write grants because they have identified a need within their organization and/or community and have devised a program or project to address that need. The program or project fits within the funder's guidelines and supports the mission of the organization seeking funding. People who get it do not have to lock themselves away for three days before a grant proposal is due. If you have a clearly defined process for responding to grant solicitations and a clear idea of your program's design, not only can you submit a cohesive proposal that will receive funding, but you can do it without going missing for 72 hours while you desperately scribble out a grant proposal and pray that you'll be funded.

 Do not let grant dollars be the only factor driving your proposal development process. In other words, do not write a grant proposal just for the money.

1. SOME QUESTIONS AND DEFINITIONS

Do you have a grants process at your organization? Who is responsible for writing your organization's grant proposals? Who is responsible for managing grant-funded programs? Is it the same person who is responsible for administration and oversight of awarded grant funds? Do you view grant writing as a fundraising activity or a form of resource development? Is there a difference between the two? Do you differentiate between proposal development, grant writing, and grants administration? Does your organization need a fundraiser, a grant writer, or a grants administrator?

These are all important questions. They will come up in some form, sooner or later, for any organization, large or small, that wants to seriously pursue grant funding for its projects. You can address these questions proactively by analyzing your organization's needs. This will enable you to anticipate many of the issues that are bound to arise, as well as the potential problems. Or you can wait and address issues as problems develop. I urge you to choose the former approach. If you do not analyze your organization's needs and devise a clear plan of operation beforehand, the result will be, at best, failure to achieve your potential. At worst it can be disastrous.

1.1 What Is a Grant?

According to the Merriam-Webster Online Dictionary, a grant is "something granted, *especially:* a gift (as of land or money) for a particular purpose." For our purposes, a grant is a monetary award given by a government agency, foundation, corporation, or other entity to another body in order to plan, implement, or operate a particular program or fund a particular project.

1.2 What Is Fundraising?

The term "fundraising" covers a host of activities designed to solicit monetary donations for an organization, project, or cause. Simply put, to fundraise means to ask for money from individuals, corporations, and foundations. This can be accomplished through direct-mail solicitation (which includes requests for money made via postal mail, telephone, and email), annual fundraising campaigns, solicitations for major gifts and planned giving, capital campaigns (for major projects, such as construction or renovation of facilities), and special fundraising events.

Fundraisers often ask donors for unrestricted donations or gifts to help with a range of projects or to fund general operating expenses. This is how gifts and grants are different. Gifts can be restricted or unrestricted. Grants are always restricted. Gifts are flexible. Grants are not. Organizations must use grant money for the explicit purpose stated in the proposal and approved by the funder in the award notification. Grant awards are bound by a contractual obligation, reporting requirements, etc. Gifts, generally, are not.

 Grants are not something for nothing. They are agreements between the funding source and the organization receiving the grant award. When an organization accepts a grant award, a contractual arrangement is created, which is both explicit and implied. The organization agrees to administer the program it has proposed, based on the interests of or needs identified by the funder in its request for proposals (RFP) or funding guidelines.

Depending on the needs and size of your organization, a single individual (usually with a job title such as "director of development" or "development officer") may be able to handle all these fundraising activities. Larger organizations may need one or several people to support each activity, with separate development officers for annual campaigns, major gifts, planned giving, and the capital campaign, not to mention a special events planner. There may also be a grant writer in the fundraising/development department.

Soliciting grant funds is often included as part of an organization's fundraising plan, but not always. Instead, an office of resource development (see section **1.3**) may oversee grant proposals, or, because grant funds are usually used for a specific project, soliciting grants may fall under the jurisdiction of the person or department in charge of the specific project.

Fundraising campaigns that raise money for an organization's general operation, rather than for a specific project, are less likely to receive grant funds. Most funders will not give to general fundraising campaigns or will not fund general operating expenses. They prefer to identify a need and give grants that address that need.

1.3 What Is Resource Development?

Some individuals and organizations view resource development and fundraising as one and the same. Others view resource development as an altogether different activity from what I like to call pure fundraising, which is described in section **1.2**.

People who work in cause-related or issue-related nonprofit and community-based organizations consider resource development to be the same as fundraising. It all involves asking for money, which often includes writing grant proposals to fund projects and programs that address the organization's specific cause.

People who work in educational institutions, particularly in higher education, are more likely to see a difference between resource development and fundraising. Many universities and colleges have offices of resource development separate from their foundation offices, which they see as the fundraising arm of the organization. But if the resource development office doesn't "raise funds," then what does it do?

Well, that's where grants come in. Those of my colleagues who consider themselves resource developers are actually what everyone else would call a grant writer. Writing grants may not be all that they do, but it forms the basis for everything else. The impetus to apply for a particular grant will come from within the resource development office. Resource development staff are in tune with the organization's mission, vision, and strategic plan. They identify suitable grant competitions that align with the current and future goals of the organization, and they develop and write the grant proposals to support those goals. If the grant proposals are funded, the result is not just a pot of cash, but new resources, programs, and funding streams for the organization. Voilà — resource development!

1.4 What Is Proposal Development?

An organization may have a person on its fundraising or resource development staff who writes grant proposals in addition to other fundraising duties. If the organization writes enough grant proposals each year, it may have a dedicated staff person who only writes grant proposals.

However, whether you write the grant proposal or not, if you are involved in any way with planning, creating, or developing grant proposals within your organization, you are part of the proposal development process. Development personnel and/or grant writers at nonprofit organizations develop proposals. Grants office personnel at colleges and universities, who may not consider themselves grant writers, more often than not assist in the proposal development process. Resource developers who do not fundraise but focus on securing grant funding for their organizations are most certainly doing proposal development. And all the other people who write grant proposals and seek grant funds for their programs — whether a pastor or parishioner at a church, a nonprofit staffer or volunteer, a K-12 principal or teacher — are engaged in proposal development. I'll discuss the process in detail in Chapter 3.

1.5 What Is Grants Administration?

Grants administration encompasses a variety of pre-award and post-award activities that involve monitoring grant proposals and grant-funded programs. Pre-award activities range from identifying funding sources, assessing the RFP and funder guidelines, and brainstorming project ideas, all the way to planning and developing programs and writing and submitting the proposal. Post-award activities include accepting the terms of the grant award, negotiating contracts, monitoring the expenditure of grant funds, preparing reports, and making sure that the grant is administered according to funder guidelines, adheres to state and federal regulations, and meets any internal requirements of the organization.

1.6 What Is a Sponsored Program?

A sponsored program is any program or project within an organization that is funded by external sources. It can be a grant program, contract, or cooperative agreement "sponsored" or funded by an outside organization. The term "sponsored program" is most commonly used in higher education and generally refers to government grant and contract funding.

1.7 What Is Research Administration?

Research administration is the equivalent of grants administration. It refers to the range of management, administrative, and financial activities that occur both pre- and post-award and that are necessary to the oversight of sponsored programs. It is another term used primarily by institutions of higher education, as well as by hospitals and research facilities.

Staff people referred to as research administrators (who work in an office of research administration) provide technical assistance to the organization's principal investigators and project directors and carry out regulatory oversight of programs. Their purpose is to ensure compliance with internal and external rules and regulations, thereby strengthening compliance awareness and promoting good stewardship of sponsored funding.

2. DETERMINING ORGANIZATIONAL CAPACITY

Now that you understand the terminology, you need to figure out where your organization fits in. The first thing your organization should do before embarking on the grants process is conduct a needs assessment. Call together your organization's administrative staff to discuss the future of the organization, determine how grants fit into the picture, and evaluate the organization's capacity to develop proposals and administer grant funds. Worksheet 1, the Organizational Capacity Questionnaire, will get you started.

WORKSHEET 1
ORGANIZATIONAL CAPACITY QUESTIONNAIRE

1. Type of organization:

   _____ State government   _____ Public college or university

   _____ Local government   _____ Private, nonprofit college or university

   _____ Special district   _____ Nonprofit organization

   _____ Indian tribe   _____ Private, profit-making organization

   _____ Independent school district   _____ Other (Specify): _____

2. How many programs does your organization support?

   _____ 5 or fewer   _____ 16 to 50

   _____ 6 to 10   _____ 51 to 100

   _____ 11 to 15   _____ Over 100

3. How many employees does your organization have?

   _____ 3 or fewer   _____ 15 to 50

   _____ 4 to 5   _____ 51 to 100

   _____ 6 to 14   _____ Over 100

4. What is your annual budget?

   _____ Less than $150,000   _____ $500,000 to $999,999

   _____ $150,000 to $299,999   _____ $1,000,000 to $4,999,999

   _____ $300,000 to $499,999   _____ $5,000,000 or more

5. What percentage of the organization's total budget is currently comprised of grant funds?

   _____ Less than 5%   _____ 21% to 35%

   _____ 5% to 10%   _____ 36% to 50%

   _____ 11% to 20%   _____ Over 50%

6. What percentage of the organization's total budget would you like to be comprised of grant funds?

   _____ Less than 5%   _____ 21% to 35%

   _____ 5% to 10%   _____ 36% to 50%

   _____ 11% to 20%   _____ Over 50%

7. How many grants do you develop/write/submit in a single year?

   _____ 5 or fewer   _____ 16 to 50

   _____ 6 to 10   _____ 51 to 100

   _____ 11 to 15   _____ Over 100

8. How many grants would you like to develop/write/submit in a single year?

_____ 5 or fewer   _____ 16 to 50

_____ 6 to 10   _____ 51 to 100

_____ 11 to 15   _____ Over 100

9. Is your organization primarily seeking grants for unrestricted operating expenses or grants to develop and/or support projects?

_____ Operating grants   _____ Project grants   _____ Both

10. Approximately how many grants will be foundation or corporate grants?

_____ 5 or fewer   _____ 16 to 25

_____ 6 to 10   _____ 26 to 50

_____ 11 to 15   _____ Over 50

11. Approximately how many grants will be state or local government grants?

_____ 5 or fewer   _____ 16 to 25

_____ 6 to 10   _____ 26 to 50

_____ 11 to 15   _____ Over 50

12. Approximately how many grants will be federal government grants?

_____ 5 or fewer   _____ 16 to 25

_____ 6 to 10   _____ 26 to 50

_____ 11 to 15   _____ Over 50

13. Will grant writing be a responsibility shared by many employees or only a select few?

_____ Many   _____ Few   How many? _____

14. If several employees will share the duty of writing grants, which department or employee will be responsible for coordinating these activities, including compliance issues?

_____

_____

15. If only one employee will possess the duty of writing grants, which department or employee will be responsible for coordinating these activities, including compliance issues?

_____

_____

16. Does the volume of grant proposals currently being generated or anticipated require the hiring of one or more staff dedicated to the organization's grants?

_____ Yes   _____ No   If yes, how many? _____

17. If a dedicated staff person(s) for grants is hired, will this individual be solely responsible for developing and writing all of the organization's grant proposals, that is, will this person serve as the organization's grant writer?

_____ Yes   _____ No

18. Will the dedicated staff person be responsible for ensuring compliance of grant-funded projects?

_____ Yes   _____ No

19. Will the dedicated staff person in cooperation with grant program staff be responsible for the financial management of awarded grant funds or will the organization's regular financial staff manage this task?

_____ Dedicated grants staff   _____ Existing financial staff

Comments: _____

_____

_____

_____

_____

_____

_____

_____

_____

_____

_____

_____

_____

_____

This questionnaire is a helpful tool for assessing your organization's capacity to competitively —

- pursue a moderate to high volume of grant funding, particularly federal grant funding, and

- administer awarded funds.

2.1 Completing the Questionnaire

The organization's CEO and/or governing body should complete Worksheet 1 with input from staff. If the CEO and the governing body complete the document separately, their responses should be consistent. This indicates that all parties share a vision of the future of the organization. If the visions differ, you will need to address this before you start developing grant proposals — you might want to schedule some strategic planning sessions or at least meet to reach an agreement on the direction everyone sees the organization moving over the next few years.

The aim of this evaluation process is to ensure you establish the best organizational structure to meet your grant-funding goals, or to "ramp up" an organization that has a more relaxed approach to pursuing grants. The process should help everyone within the organization distinguish his or her roles and responsibilities. Focus on the needs of the organization, current and future. (You may need to adapt the questions to your particular situation.)

2.2 Assessing the Data Collected

Your answers to the questions on Worksheet 1 can determine where you will look for funds or what you might be eligible for.

- *Question 1:* The type of organization is important because it determines the kind of grants for which you will be eligible to apply. As you will see in Chapter 2, foundation grants are generally available only to nonprofit organizations, meaning those organizations that possess 501(c)(3) tax-exempt status. Foundations also commonly award grants to public and private K-12 school districts, as well as public and private colleges and universities, even if they don't have a separate 501(c)(3) arm, because these institutions do not make a profit and they do serve the public good. State and local governments, special districts, and Indian tribal governments will not find many foundations willing to give them grant money. Instead, they will submit most of their grant applications to the federal government. Foundations will also not give to profit-making organizations.

  All the organizations listed in Question 1 can pursue federal government grants. They may not be eligible to apply for every federal grant, but the federal government does offer a number of grant programs for each type of organization.

- *Question 2:* An organization that supports many programs will have more funding options than an organization that runs only a couple of programs.

- *Question 3:* The more employees your organization has, the more staff available to develop and write grant proposals. This, in turn, will require strict internal control of the grants process and centralized monitoring of grants submitted and grants awarded.

- *Questions 4 to 6:* Your organization's annual budget, and the current and potential impact on the organization's bottom line, will inform your decisions about the type and dollar amount of grants you apply for, what changes in personnel are necessary to reach or maintain your desired status, and what internal processes you need to implement to ensure the highest program integrity for grant funds received.

- *Questions 7 to 8:* These questions ask you to assess current and desired output, which should encourage you to reflect on how the organization's current capacity for handling grants will have to change to reach the desired output.

- *Questions 9 to 12:* These questions ask you to assess the organization's capacity for developing, writing, submitting, and administering a variety of grant types. Operating grants are in far shorter supply than project grants, so an organization primarily seeking operating grants will not be applying for nearly as many grants as an organization seeking project grants. It is also much less work to prepare an operating grant application.

Foundation and corporate grants not only require less information from applicants in terms of the actual proposal, but they also require much less monitoring once awarded.

State and local government grants vary widely in their application requirements as well as in the extent of monitoring; however, it is fair to say that organizations will not be able to take a relaxed approach to preparing state and local grant proposals for submission, nor to monitoring them once grant funds are awarded.

Federal grants require the most effort for preparing proposals and have the strictest guidelines for monitoring. Any organization that has five or more multiyear federal awards *must* designate a single staff person or create a centralized grants office to ensure that the organization is in full compliance with federal government programs and financial rules and regulations.

- *Question 13:* The answer to this question will be informed by the answers to all the questions that came before it. Think about the number of programs your organization operates, the diversity of the programs, and the number and types of grants that your organization plans to write. Does it make more sense to have designated staff within each program area be responsible for developing and writing grants within their area, or would the organization be better served by hiring a grant writer? Do current staff have the time to add substantial amounts of grant writing to their list of job duties? Would hiring one grant writer be adequate to handle the anticipated workload?

- *Questions 14 to 18:* If more than one individual or office is involved in writing grants within a single organization, who will serve as the single point of contact or centralized office to coordinate all of the organization's grants activities and ensure internal and external compliance, both before proposals are submitted and after proposals are funded?

- *Question 19:* The person who ensures compliance with grant rules and regulations may or may not also deal with the financial management of grant awards. Consider whether your organization's staff has the capacity to handle this duty. Many organizations will hire a grants accountant who deals solely with grant funds (Sample 3 in Chapter 3 includes a job description for a grants accountant). This person may be housed in either the centralized grants office or in the finance office of the organization. If your organization has been awarded five or more federal grants, particularly multiyear grants, I would strongly recommend that you hire a grants accountant.

2

WHAT IS A GRANT AND WHERE CAN WE GET ONE?
LEARNING THE BASICS OF GRANTSMANSHIP

As mentioned in Chapter 1, a grant is a monetary award given by a government agency, foundation, corporation, or other entity to fund a particular project or program.

As a general rule, grants are given to organizations as opposed to individuals, and these organizations are usually required to have 501(c)(3) tax-exempt status (an Internal Revenue Service designation) to be eligible for funding. This is not to say that grants are never given to individuals. They are, but usually under very limited circumstances. This book will not address grants to individuals. Grants are also occasionally made to profit-making entities, but, overwhelmingly, funders require that organizations receiving grant funds have nonprofit status.

The two main sources of funds are the federal government and foundations. Organizations other than the federal government or foundations also give grants. State and city governments often hold grant competitions. Many corporations have corporate giving programs, as well. However, the easiest and most accessible sources of grant funding are the federal government and foundations.

By "easy" I do not mean to imply that seeking out and procuring grant funds from external sources is a simple task. It's not. The process can be complicated and confusing. By "easy and accessible" I mean that the federal government, through its numerous agencies, administers hundreds of grant programs by means of an organized, competitive grants process. Many of these grant programs have been around for several decades and are cyclical. Though the amount of funding may change from one cycle to the next, these programs were designed to address a specific problem or issue, and they rarely deviate from their original intent. As a result, these programs are easy to plan for and predictable.

 Most grant funding is consistent. A large number of grant competitions are held cyclically, which makes the act of writing a grant proposal a predictable activity that you can plan for well in advance of a proposal's due date.

1. WHERE DO YOU GO TO LEARN ABOUT GRANT PROGRAMS?

The first step to success in the grants process is to research the guidelines of federal grant programs and foundations to determine which programs and/or funders are suitable matches for your organization. There are numerous resources available to groups engaged in seeking grants and writing proposals. When used consistently, they will help you discover a number of potential sources of funding. First, let's look at the most commonly used re-sources for finding and understanding federal grant programs.

1.1 Federal Government Grants

In 2008, the federal government distributed more than $574.7 billion, accounting for 20.6 percent of federal government expenditures, in the form of grants to governmental units and nonprofit entities (according to the US Census Bureau's *Consolidated Federal Funds Report for Fiscal Year 2008*). There are 26 federal agencies that award grant funds through more than 1,000 programs. These are the most useful resources for finding information on these programs:

- *Catalog of Federal Domestic Assistance (CFDA)*
- Federal Register
- Federal agency websites
- Grants.gov

1.1a Catalog of Federal Domestic Assistance (CFDA)

The *Catalog of Federal Domestic Assistance* is a publication of the federal government. It lists all financial and service-related programs sponsored by the United States government through its various agencies that are available to state and local governments, US territories, federally recognized Indian tribal governments, nonprofit and for-profit organizations, and individuals. It includes federal grant programs.

Through fiscal year 2003, the CFDA was published annually by the General Services Administration (GSA) and distributed to designated recipients, such as public libraries, at no cost. In 2004, in accordance with the Government Paperwork Elimination Act, the GSA discontinued printing and distributing free copies of the CFDA in favor of electronic dissemination via the CFDA website on the Internet, located at www.cfda.gov. You can download the CFDA and print it in its entirety. The 2008 version is a lengthy 2,205 pages! It makes more sense to wade through the CFDA online.

Information in the CFDA is arranged in a user-friendly, logical format. The programs are divided into 15 types of federal assistance, making for an organized, easy-to-browse website. The CFDA classification system is shown in Table 1.

Remember, the CFDA is a comprehensive database of all federal programs. When researching grant programs that your organization may be eligible for, you should focus on Formula Grants and Project Grants. The website will help you identify federal grant programs for which you may be eligible, but you cannot apply for grants through the website (see section **1** of Chapter 6 for information on how to apply).

There are several ways to conduct a search of the CFDA. You may search by typing a "Keyword or Program Number" into the search field and further narrowing your search by using the "Select Assistance Type"

TABLE 1
CFDA — TYPES OF ASSISTANCE

A. Formula Grants	Allocations of money to states or their subdivisions in accordance with distribution formulas prescribed by law or administrative regulation, for activities of a continuing nature not confined to a specific project.
B. Project Grants	The funding, for fixed or known periods, of specific projects. Project grants can include fellowships, scholarships, research grants, training grants, traineeships, experimental and demonstration grants, evaluation grants, planning grants, technical assistance grants, survey grants, and construction grants.
C. Direct Payments for Specified Use	Financial assistance from the federal government provided directly to individuals, private firms, and other private institutions to encourage or subsidize a particular activity by conditioning the receipt of the assistance on a particular performance by the recipient. This does not include solicited contracts for the procurement of goods and services for the federal government.
D. Direct Payments with Unrestricted Use	Financial assistance from the federal government provided directly to beneficiaries who satisfy federal eligibility requirements with no restrictions being imposed on the recipient as to how the money is spent. Included are payments under retirement, pension, and compensatory programs.
E. Direct Loans	Financial assistance provided through the lending of federal monies for a specific period of time, with a reasonable expectation of repayment. Such loans may or may not require the payment of interest.
F. Guaranteed/Insured Loans	Programs in which the federal government makes an arrangement to indemnify a lender against part or all of any defaults by those responsible for repayment of loans.
G. Insurance	Financial assistance provided to assure reimbursement for losses sustained under specified conditions. Coverage may be provided directly by the federal government or through private carriers and may or may not involve the payment of premiums.
H. Sale, Exchange, or Donation of Property and Goods	Programs which provide for the sale, exchange, or donation of federal real property, personal property, commodities, and other goods including land, buildings, equipment, food, and drugs. This does not include the loan of, use of, or access to federal facilities or property.
I. Use of Property, Facilities, and Equipment	Programs which provide for the loan of, use of, or access to federal facilities or property wherein the federally owned facilities or property do not remain in the possession of the recipient of the assistance.

TABLE 1 — CONTINUED

J. Provision of Specialized Services	Programs that provide federal personnel directly to perform certain tasks for the benefit of communities or individuals. These services may be performed in conjunction with nonfederal personnel, but they involve more than consultation, advice, or counseling.
K. Advisory Services and Counseling	Programs which provide federal specialists to consult, advise, or counsel communities or individuals to include conferences, workshops, or personal contacts. This may involve the use of published information, but only in a secondary capacity.
L. Dissemination of Technical Information	Programs that provide for the publication and distribution of information or data of a specialized or technical nature, frequently through clearinghouses or libraries. This does not include conventional public information services designed for general public consumption.
M. Training	Programs that provide instructional activities conducted directly by a federal agency for individuals not employed by the federal government.
N. Investigation of Complaints	Federal administrative agency activities that are initiated in response to requests, either formal or informal, to examine or investigate claims of violations of federal statutes, policies, or procedure. The origination of such claims must come from outside the federal government.
O. Federal Employment	Programs that reflect the government-wide responsibilities of the Office of Personnel Management in the recruitment and hiring of federal civilian agency personnel.

drop down menu, which allows you to choose from among the fifteen types of federal assistance detailed in Table 1. You may also use the "Select Assistance Type" feature without entering a "Keyword or Program Number."

The CFDA website also offers an "Advanced Search Form" link as well as the ability to "Find Programs by Number" and "Find Programs by Agency." As with numerous other websites, the CFDA's search features are sophisticated and fairly self-explanatory. Once you find a program that interests you, simply follow the links to obtain additional information about the program. A program listing in the CFDA (an example of which is shown in Sample 1) provides a wealth of information to potential applicants.

1.1b Federal Register

The *Federal Register* is published daily Monday through Friday, excluding holidays, by the National Archives and Records Administration, in partnership with the Government Printing Office. The *Federal Register* is organized into four categories:

- *Presidential documents:* Includes executive orders and proclamations
- *Rules and regulations:* Includes policy statements and interpretations of federal agency rules and regulations
- *Proposed rules:* Includes petitions and proposals for new rules and regulations

- *Notices:* Includes schedules for public meetings and hearings, notices of grant competitions and requests for proposals, and administrative orders

This last category is the only one with which we need to concern ourselves. It is in this section that federal agencies inform the public about federal grant competitions through a Notice of Funding Availability (NOFA) or a Request for Proposals (RFP). Like the *CFDA*, the *Federal Register* is available online at www.gpoaccess.gov/fr/index.html.

On this website you can search all issues of the *Federal Register* dating back to January 1, 1994. In the beginning, you may want to search the *Federal Register* for grant announcements each day. As you become more familiar with the online system, you can search once a week for the past week's notices. Because the daily *Federal Register* can be very long, it is not necessary to examine the entire document. Instead, search only each day's "Contents" page.

Using the "Advanced Search" link on the *Federal Register* website, you can narrow your search using a variety of criteria. To access only the table of contents for a specific date, simply pick a volume (a single volume represents a year), select the section called "Contents and Preliminary Pages," and search by issue date by selecting "ON" and typing in the exact date. You may also search a week's worth of *Federal Register* by selecting "Date Range" and typing in a start date and end date.

Once you have submitted your search criteria, your results page will appear, giving you a list of hits. Select the "Contents" result, which is offered in both HTML and PDF formats. This will take you to the table of contents of the selected day's *Federal Register*, which lists each federal agency in alphabetical order.

All documents in each issue are listed under the agency to which they pertain and are sorted according to the *Federal Register*'s four main categories. If you are looking for grant announcements, you should pay attention to the "Notices" sections. When you spot them, look further to determine whether there is an announcement of funding availability. If you do see an announcement for grant funding that interests you, make a note of the program name, go back to the search page, deselect "Contents and Preliminary Pages," enter the specific date of the *Federal Register* in which the announcement was located, and type the name of the grant program into the search box. This will take you directly to the *Federal Register* announcement of the specific grant program for which you are looking.

The most important thing to remember is that if you find a grant competition that has been announced in the *Federal Register*, you have a fairly narrow window of opportunity to design a program, complete a grant proposal, and submit your application. Unlike the *CFDA*, which merely provides you with a list of grant programs and basic information on each program, the *Federal Register* tells you that a particular program is currently accepting applications and outlines everything that you must do to complete the application process. The *Federal Register* notice will give specific instructions on what goes into each application. It may also provide questions that potential grantees are required to address, with instructions on how to deal with these questions.

Some federal agencies will not go into such detail in their *Federal Register* notices, but instead will refer you to the specific agency sponsoring the grant program. Of course, as with everything else, you will find that this

SAMPLE 1
CFDA PROGRAM NOTICE

Minority Science and Engineering Improvement
MSEIP
Number: 84.120
Agency: Department of Education
Office: Office Of Postsecondary Education

PROGRAM INFORMATION

Authorization (040):

Higher Education Act of 1965, as amended, Executive Order Title III, Part E, Subpart 1.

Objectives (050):

To (1) Effect long-range improvement in science and engineering education at predominantly minority institutions and (2) increase the participation of underrepresented ethnic minorities, particularly minority women, in scientific and technological careers.

Types of Assistance (060):

PROJECT GRANTS

Uses and Use Restrictions (070):

The program funds are generally used to implement design projects, institutional projects, and cooperative projects. The program also supports special projects designed to provide or improve support to accredited nonprofit colleges, universities, and professional scientific organizations for a broad range of activities that address specific barriers that eliminate or reduce the entry of minorities into science and technology fields. Grant funds may be used for paying costs necessary for improving and maintaining high quality science and engineering education programs in minority postsecondary institutions, including salaries and wages, equipment and instructional materials and supplies, travel related to the project activities, faculty development, and other direct and indirect costs. This program is subject to non-supplanting requirements and must use a restricted indirect cost rate which is referenced under 34 CFR 76.564-76.569. For assistance call the Office of the Chief Financial Officer/Indirect Cost Group on (202) 377-3838.

Eligibility Requirements (080)

Applicant Eligibility (081):
Private and public nonprofit accredited institutions of higher education that award baccalaureate degrees; and are minority institutions; public or private nonprofit institutions of higher education that award associate degrees, and are minority institutions that have a curriculum that includes science or engineering subjects; and enters into a partnership with public or private nonprofit institutions of higher education that award baccalaureate degrees in science or engineering. Applications may also be submitted by nonprofit science-oriented organizations, professional scientific societies, and institutions of higher education that award baccalaureate degrees, that provide a needed service to a group of minority institutions; or provide in-service training for project directors, scientists, and engineers from minority institutions; or consortia of organizations, that provide needed services to

one or more minority institutions, the membership of which may include: institutions of higher education which have a curriculum in science and engineering; institutions of higher education that have graduate or professional programs in science or engineering; research laboratories of, or under contract with the Department of Energy; private organizations that have science and engineering facilities; or quasi-governmental entities that have a significant scientific or engineering mission.

Beneficiary Eligibility (082):
Private or public accredited 4-year institutions of higher education whose total enrollments are predominantly (50 percent or more) American Indian; Alaskan Native; Black (not of Hispanic origin); Hispanic (including persons of Mexican, Puerto Rican, Cuban, and Central or South American origin); Pacific Islander; or any combination of these or other ethnic minorities who are underrepresented in science and engineering. Also, 2- year private or public accredited minority (see description of minority above) institutions that have curricula in science or engineering and have formed a partnership with a 4-year institution.

Credentials/Documentation (083):
Institutions must provide the information necessary to establish their eligibility for participation in MSEIP. The data on enrollment furnished to the Office for Civil Rights to satisfy requirements for the "Fall Enrollment and Compliance Report of Institutions of Higher Education" are acceptable. Applications must be signed by the project director(s), the relevant department head(s), and by an authorized organizational official. This program is excluded from coverage under OMB Circular No. A-87.

Application and Award Process (090)

Preapplication Coordination (091):
An applicant should consult the office or official designated as the single point of contact in his or her State for more information on the process the State requires to be followed in applying for assistance, if the State has selected the program for review. Environmental impact information is not required for this program. This program is eligible for coverage under E.O. 12372, "Intergovernmental Review of Federal Programs." An applicant should consult the office or official designated as the single point of contact in his or her State for more information on the process the State requires to be followed in applying for assistance, if the State has selected the program for review.

Application Procedures (092):
OMB Circular No. A-102 applies to this program. OMB Circular No. A-110 applies to this program. An eligible institution may submit a proposal for funding of a planned project and proposed amount of the grant when announcement of a new competition appears in the Federal Register. See 34 CFR 637 and the specific program guidelines. Application forms are available from the MSEIP.

Award Procedure (093):
Panels of outside experts with knowledge of the fields covered by the application review all applications. Grants awards are recommended to the Secretary by the program office, in the order of merit.

Deadlines (094):
Contact the headquarters or regional office, as appropriate, for application deadlines.

Range of Approval/Disapproval Time (095):
From 3 to 6 months.

Appeals (096):
Not Applicable.

Renewals (097):
Awards may be renewed for up to 2 years, renewals subject to the availability of appropriations.

Assistance Consideration (100)

Formula and Matching Requirements (101):
This program has no statutory formula.

This program has no matching requirements.

This program does not have MOE requirements.

Length and Time Phasing of Assistance (102):
One to three years. Funds are awarded annually and disbursed as required. Renewals are subject to the availability of appropriations. See the following for information on how assistance is awarded/released: Electronic transfer.

Post Assistance Requirements (110)

Reports (111):
The program requires interim performance reports from directors of projects having duration of more than one year at the end of each budget year's activities. A substantive performance and financial report is required within 90 days upon completion of the project for all funded projects. Cash reports are not applicable. Progress reports are not applicable. Expenditure reports are not applicable. Performance monitoring is not applicable.

Audits (112):
This program is excluded from coverage under OMB Circular No. A-133. Compliance with standard Department of Education requirements.

Records (113):
Grantees are required to maintain standard programmatic and financial records. Records are subject to inspection during the life of the grant and for three years thereafter.

Financial Information (120)

Account Identification (121):
91-0201-0-1-502.

Obligations (122):
(Project Grants) FY 08 $8,577,487; FY 09 est $8,577,000; FY 10 est $9,006,000

Range and Average of Financial Assistance (123):
To be determined.

Program Accomplishments (130):
Fiscal Year 2008: For FY 2008, approximately 16 new awards and 51 continuation awards were made. Fiscal Year 2009: Seventeen new awards and 38 continuation awards are expected to be made in FY 2009. Fiscal Year 2010: Nineteen new awards and 33 continuation awards are expected to be made in FY 2010.

Regulations, Guidelines, and Literature (140):
34 CFR 637 and the Education Department General Administrative Regulations.

Information Contacts (150)

Regional or Local Office (151) :
None.

Headquarters Office (152):
Bernadette Hence Office of Postsecondary Education, Institutional Development and Undergraduate Education Service, Department of Education, 400 Maryland Ave. S.W., Washington, District of Columbia 20202 Email: bernadette.hence@ed.gov Phone: (202) 219-7038.

Website Address (153):
http://www.ed.gov/programs/iduesmsi/ .

Related Programs (160):
84.031 Higher Education_Institutional Aid; 84.116 Fund for the Improvement of Postsecondary Education

Examples of Funded Projects (170):
Fiscal Year 2008: (1) A project is providing state-of- the-art training to minority students in field and laboratory studies dealing with water quality, and educating students on the benefits of using an interdisciplinary approach to solving environmental problems. (2) A project has a summer science program designed to improve access of pre-college (8th and 9th grade) minority students to careers in science and engineering. Integrated, hands-on curriculum in biology, physical science, mathematics, and computer technology is offered. (3) A project is a consortium of five minority serving community colleges across the nation and two engineering schools whose purpose is to share resources and strategies in order to increase the number of bilingual engineers and strengthen the educational pipeline from pre-college through engineering school. (4) One project is to establish a computer laboratory in science and mathematics. Fiscal Year 2009: No Current Data Available Fiscal Year 2010: No Current Data Available

Criteria for Selecting Proposals (180):
Decisions are based primarily on the scientific and educational merits of described activities and conformance with the objectives of the program. Priority is given to applicants which have not previously received funding from the Minority Science Improvement Program and to previous grantees with a proven record of success, as well as to proposals that contribute to achieving balance among projects with respect to geographic region, academic discipline and project type.

information is available online. Go to the website of the federal agency sponsoring the program that interests you, where you can find and download the application package.

1.1c Federal agency websites

Federal agency websites are among the very best places to find information on grant programs. They have always been my first choice. Even if you don't know exactly what program you are looking for, you can always target a federal agency or agencies that would logically offer grant programs that relate to your organization's purpose.

Each agency website is different, of course, but they all include a link to information on grant programs sponsored by the particular agency. Often a potential grantee can glean a great deal more about programs by visiting the sponsoring agency's website than by scrolling through the CFDA and the *Federal Register*. For example, the US Department of Education has a separate page for each of its grant programs where applicants can learn about the history of a program, its authorizing legislation, which organizations were awarded funding in the last grant competition, how much each grantee received, and the number of potential new awards to be given. Potential applicants can also download the current application package. Some federal agency websites also will provide a synopsis of previously funded projects.

1.1d Grants.gov

Established in the fall of 2004, Grants.gov (www.grants.gov), serves as a single point of contact for all federal government grant programs. The federal government has created what it refers to as a "unified electronic storefront" to facilitate all interactions between federal agencies and grant seekers, applicants, and awardees. Grants.gov is a one-stop source where potential applicants can search for grant opportunities from every federal agency and apply electronically to those programs.

The site permits users to find and access currently open competitions — as well as those that have closed — with the click of a mouse, all on a single website. As a result, you do not have to conduct long, tedious searches using the *Federal Register* — which is particularly helpful if you are unsure about what you are looking for.

There are numerous ways to conduct a Grants.gov search. When you know specifically what you are looking for, use "Basic Search" or "Advanced Search." With "Basic Search," applicants can search by keyword, Funding Opportunity number, or CFDA number. "Advanced Search" allows you to search by keyword; open, closed, or archived opportunities; funding opportunity number; CFDA number; date; eligibility; activity; or agency. When you're unsure about what type of grant program you're looking for, browse by category or agency.

Grants.gov has only been around for a short period of time, but it has proven to be an invaluable research tool for anyone seeking information on federal grant programs, not to mention the primary means of submission for most federal grant applications.

1.2 Foundation Grants

The second-largest source of grant funding awarded in the United States is foundations. According to the Foundation Center (www.foundationcenter.org), "a foundation is an entity that is established as a nonprofit corporation or a charitable trust, with a principal purpose of making grants to unrelated organizations or institutions."

Basically, a foundation is an independent, nonprofit, grant-making organization. Again, according to the Foundation Center, there were more than 75,187 grantmaking foundations in the United States in 2007, and they distributed $45.6 billion in funding in 2008. But who are they? How do you find them? Will they give money to your organization?

1.2a Foundation directories

As simple and old-fashioned as it sounds, the first place to start looking for foundation grants is your local library. In the reference section, there is likely to be one or more directories and other publications with a listing of foundations. The focus of each directory could be based on any number of systems for collecting and categorizing the information — for example, there could be a Directory of Louisiana Foundations, a Directory of Grantmakers in Education, Grants for Youth Services, etc. Do not just look for local or state foundation directories. There are numerous directories that compile a list of foundations from around the country, arranged by state and indexed by causes supported, amount of money given, etc.

1.2b Internet resources

The Internet, as I mentioned before, is my favorite method of research. I always start there, at least to conduct preliminary research. Several websites provide information on grants, on grant writing, and on nongovernment sources of funding for nonprofits, from family foundations to corporate foundations. There are a number of local organizations dedicated to nonprofit management and that publish their own foundation directories, which are available not just in print, but also online. Many foundations have their own web pages where you can learn about the history of the foundation, find out about its grant programs, and frequently, these days, apply online.

Corporations often have established philanthropic arms to serve the community. Visit corporate home pages and you will likely find links to "Giving," "Community," or "Foundation" pages, which will give you information on the company's grant programs.

1.2c The Foundation Center

The Foundation Center is the preeminent resource for all information related to foundations in the United States. Through its website (www.foundationcenter.org), the center offers access to a database of 98,000 grantmakers and allows users to browse information on the more than 1.7 million grants these organizations have given to the nonprofit sector. As well, there is a database of thousands of IRS Form 990s (see section **2.2c**). You can search these records using a number of criteria. A great deal of the information on the Foundation Center's website is free of charge, although some information is available by subscription only.

The center publishes dozens of books, directories, guides, and reports on the nonprofit sector each year. Five Foundation Center libraries/learning centers and 400 Cooperating Collections (information centers) across the United States offer free access to all the center's publications. The center also offers online tutorials, as well as live seminars and workshops, which provide training on aspects of the grants process from research of funding sources to proposal writing. There is likely either a Foundation Center library or Cooperating Collection in a city near you. The center is the ultimate resource for grant seekers interested in pursuing foundation grants.

 When funding agencies are holding RFP workshops (also known as technical assistance trainings or bidders' conferences) for writing their proposals, attend. Some of these workshops are mandatory for applicants. Yes, the more experience you have with grants, the less interesting and/or helpful these workshops will be. However, they do give you a chance to check out the competition. Also, the funder may share a tidbit of information that you would not receive otherwise.

1.2d The Chronicle of Philanthropy

Like the Foundation Center, *The Chronicle of Philanthropy* is the preeminent resource of its kind in the country. It bills itself as "the newspaper of the nonprofit world" and is available in print and online at www.philanthropy.com, with 24 issues per year.

The Chronicle of Philanthropy is full of timely articles covering subjects of interest to nonprofit professionals. It covers the world of philanthropy and fundraising, including grantsmanship. You will find information on funders, open grant competitions, recent grant awards made to nonprofit organizations, available workshops and training sessions held by various organizations across the country, as well as an abundance of other resources.

The Chronicle of Philanthropy is not free, and there is limited information available on the website to nonsubscribers. A subscription to the print version will give you full access to the website. An online-only subscription is also available.

1.2e Other sources

There are a number of other sources of information on finding and applying for grants — directories, paper and email newsletters, websites — all designed to aid people who are in the business of researching sources of grant funding. Some are of a higher quality than others. Some are more helpful than others. They are organized based on any number of criteria — cause-based funding, federal funding, foundation grants, or any combination of these and other criteria. Some are free. Most require you pay or subscribe in order to access all the information they provide. You will also find that some track and compile information on federal legislation that affects grant funding, which can be very helpful as a planning tool.

My advice to beginners would be to use the other methods described in this chapter to research funding sources first. Not only are they the most commonly used techniques, but they are also free. They will give you an idea of what is out there to meet the needs of your organization. Initially you may find that these methods of researching grant funding are time-consuming, but with some experience, your research should become more efficient.

If you find these sources to be inadequate or too cumbersome, think about subscribing to one of the services that will research and compile the information for you. Do your research before committing, as subscriptions to these resources can be expensive. Find the source that will most closely meet your needs. Many services will offer a few issues of a newsletter at no cost, or free access to a grants database for a limited time, to help you make a decision about subscribing. Take advantage of these offers to find the best and most economical research tool for your organization.

(See the list of resources on the CD-ROM that accompanies this book.)

2. RESEARCHING YOUR FUNDING SOURCE

Now that you know where to go to learn about sources of grant funding, you need to know how to research a funding source and/or grant program to determine whether or not to make an application for funding.

2.1 Federal Government Grants

When it comes to federal government grants, the process has been so perfected, streamlined, and duplicated across agencies that it is fairly easy to determine exactly what is expected of an organization that applies for, and is awarded, grant funds. There are three basic issues to address when deciding whether or not to apply for funding:

- *Eligibility:* Make sure that your organization is among the types listed as eligible to apply for and receive funding.

- *Size of award:* Make sure that the estimated amount of each grant award, or the cap placed on each award, is sufficient to carry out program activities. Do not commit to carry out a program when you know that the grant will not provide enough funding to do the job adequately.

- *Project focus:* Make sure that the focus of the funder's grant program and the focus of your organization and its proposed project complement each other. You do not want to create a project that is inconsistent with the vision, mission, and needs of your organization just to get funding. If you propose a project outside the funder's area of interest,

your grant will not be funded and you will have wasted the time spent writing the application.

 Only apply for those grants that match the needs of your organization and the population it serves with the vision, mission, and goals of the funder.

2.2 Foundation Grants

It can be more difficult to tease out the information necessary to make a decision about whether or not to apply for foundation grants. Unfortunately, the 75,000 foundations around the country are not linked by a common set of rules, a common application form, or a common procedure to apply for funding. However, in almost every case, there are three documents you will need from each foundation to help you decide whether to submit a grant proposal:

- Funding guidelines

- Annual reports

- Information returns (IRS Form 990)

2.2a Funding guidelines

If you are lucky, the foundation that you are interested in has its own website. On that website, you should find the foundation's funding guidelines. Use these guidelines to determine the following information:

- *Your organization's eligibility to apply for funds.* This includes not only what types of organizations can apply, but also whether there are any geographic or other restrictions on applicants. It is not uncommon for family and corporate foundations to limit grants to organizations located in the region, state, city, or town in which the company does business.

- *The foundation's funding priorities.* Foundations do not fund each and every good cause. That would be an impossible task. Instead they focus on only a few causes and target their resources in an effort to "fix" a particular problem. In this way, foundations and corporate giving programs limit their philanthropic efforts to the interest(s) of their founder or board members, or closely ally their priorities with their business areas or other special areas of interest.

- *The activities that the foundation will fund, as well as those it will not fund.* It is common for foundations to list what types of activities they will and, most importantly, will *not* fund. For example, a foundation that supports education may give money to fund a program that provides tutoring and mentoring to low-income students, but it may *not* give to scholarship funds or endowments. A foundation's guidelines will let you know what restrictions it is placing on the use of its funds.

- *The size of the grant award.* If a foundation places a cap of $25,000 on its grant awards and you know that you need $50,000 to run a particular program, you can either apply for the funds with a disclosure to the foundation that its grant award will cover only 50 percent of the program's costs and that you will seek the balance from other sources, or not apply for the funding at all, knowing that it is insufficient to run the program. You should never give a funder the impression that its grant award will

fully fund a program or provide a service when you know that it will not.

2.2b Annual reports

A foundation's annual report is another great source of information on its grant programs. The annual report generally contains the history of the foundation and its programs; a budget from the current year showing how and where the foundation spent its money; and often a list of funded grants, including details of amounts awarded and descriptions of the organizations and programs that received funding that year. The annual report is also the place where many foundations will print their funding guidelines and describe their application process.

2.2c Information returns (IRS Form 990)

The Internal Revenue Service (IRS) requires that Form 990, entitled "Return of Organization Exempt from Income Tax," be filed each year by tax-exempt organizations (other than private foundations) whose annual receipts are $25,000 per year or more. This form is not actually a tax return, as it is commonly called, because the organizations that file it do not pay taxes. It is, in fact, an information return.

Form 990 is the main reporting form for nonprofits. It provides information that enables state and federal government agencies to enforce the laws that govern nonprofits. It also provides a great deal of information about the filing organization's financial status, including its financial viability, sources of income, and methods of distributing its resources. The information contained in Form 990 is the bulk of the financial information contained in the annual report.

As a grant seeker, you are concerned with the portion of Form 990 that details how the foundation distributes its resources. You are looking for any information about which organizations the foundation supported with grants and how much these organizations received. You can use Form 990 in lieu of funder guidelines or an annual report — or in addition to them — in your search for information on a public charity's grant-making activities. If funders fill the form out adequately and thoroughly, they can use 990s to tell the public what types of causes its grants support, how its application process works, who has received grant awards in the past year, and how much each grantee received.

You can obtain a copy of an organization's Form 990 from the IRS via mail, directly from the public charity for a reasonable fee, or on the Internet from the online databases GuideStar (www.guidestar.org), and Noza (www.noza990pf.com), or from The Foundation Center's website.

2.3 Contacting the Funding Source

The final step when researching your funding source is to consider contacting the funder. All federal grant programs, because they are so large, are assigned one or more program officers. The federal government encourages all potential grantees to contact the appropriate program officer, ask questions, and seek clarification on grant programs. This is also an opportunity to introduce your organization to the funding agency and develop contacts with people who can be a great deal of help to you in navigating the federal grants process.

A great number of foundations encourage potential grantees to make contact with foundation program officers. There are also foundations that discourage direct communication with potential grantees. Before you

decide to contact foundation personnel, do all the preliminary research that you can. Visit the foundation's web page. Research the foundation in directories of grant makers; seek out a copy of the funder guidelines, annual report, and Form 990. A foundation's written materials will often state whether it entertains questions from grant seekers. If you cannot find anything that discourages contact, give the foundation a call. Be polite. Be prepared with questions so you do not waste the program officer's time. Also be aware that some foundations will decline to speak with you at length and may simply refer you to their prepared materials.

If you are unable to obtain funder guidelines, an annual report, or any helpful information about a foundation's grant-making efforts, you could write to the organization to request information (see Sample 2 for a model letter).

2.4 Compiling Your Research

Use a Funder Data Sheet (see Worksheet 2) to record information you obtain through your research of federal grant programs or foundations' funding guidelines, annual reports, and Form 990s, as well as in your conversation with a funder, whether by phone or in person. In fundraising circles, a form such as this is referred to as a *Prospect Worksheet*. This form can be adapted to your organization's needs.

3. DECIDING TO APPLY FOR GRANT FUNDING

Throughout this chapter, I have described where and how you can find information on funders and grant programs to determine whether or not a particular grant program will be a good fit for your organization. I stated the

The Youth Center
4567 ABC Road
Anywhere, OK 73456

July 15, 2009

Ms. Susan McDaniels, President
McDaniels Family Foundation
1234 XYZ Boulevard
Anywhere, OK 73123

Dear Ms. McDaniels:

The Youth Center would like to propose a project to aid runaway and troubled teens in the county.
The "Runaway and Troubled Teens Project" complements the focus of the McDaniels Family Foundation
as demonstrated by *(previously funded grants/information obtained on your website/other)*. The
commitment of the McDaniels Family Foundation to assisting troubled youth fits with the Youth Center's
mission to provide social services to the many troubled youth and families of the county.

I would like to request current information on your grant programs and policies, including a copy of your
annual report, funding guidelines, and application.

Please add our organization to your mailing list for future publications.

Thank you for your assistance.

Sincerely,

Marjorie Jones

Ms. Marjorie Jones, Director
(800) 123-4567

WORKSHEET 2
FUNDER DATA SHEET

FUNDER CONTACT INFORMATION

Name of funding agency: _____

Contact person/Program Officer: _____

Address: _____

_____

Telephone: _____

Fax: _____

Email: _____

Website: _____

GENERAL FUNDER DATA/FUNDING GUIDELINES

Funding Priorities: _____

_____

Geographic area(s) served: _____

_____

Total assets: _____

Total number of grants awarded: _____

Number of new grant awards: _____   Number of continuation awards: _____

Total dollar amount of grants paid: _____

Average dollar amount/Range of all grant awards: _____

Meet eligibility requirements: _____ Yes   _____ No

Duration of awards: _____ One-time award   _____ Multiyear awards

Application deadline(s): _____

Other eligibility requirements/Comments: _____

_____

_____

_____

SPECIFIC GRANT PROGRAM INFORMATION

Name of grant program: _____

Program purpose: _____

_____

Population served by grant program: _____

Number of program awards: _____

Average amount/Range of program awards: _____

Application deadline: _____

Other eligibility requirements/Comments: _____

_____

_____

APPLICATION REQUIREMENTS

_____ Application form(s)   _____ Preliminary proposal

_____ Letter of inquiry/Intent   _____ Formal proposal

Comments: _____

_____

_____

SOURCES OF INFORMATION

_____ Federal Register Notice/RFP/Other   Date: _____

_____ Funder Guidelines   Date: _____

_____ Annual Report   Year: _____

_____ IRS Form 990   Year: _____

_____ Funding Agency Website   List: _____

_____ Foundation Directory/Other   List: _____

_____ Contact with Funding Agency   Name: _____

---

three basic issues to address when deciding whether or not to apply for funding:

- Your organization's eligibility

- Amount of the grant award

- Extent to which the focus of your organization's project and the focus of the funder complement each other

Because the theme of this book *is* the process, I want to make sure that I present an organized and methodical process for pursuing grant funding. After conducting all the research, compiling a Funder Data Sheet, selecting potential funders, and assessing the basics, you think, "Eligibility … ✓; size of the grant award … ✓; compatibility of project focus … ✓. Let's apply!"

Not so fast … What else does your organization need to consider when contemplating whether or not to apply for grant funding? A lot! The definition of "a lot" will vary depending on what type of grant you are applying for, which goes hand in hand with the nature of the programs or projects you are seeking to fund.

3.1 Funder Restrictions and Organizational Ability

There are two more criteria you need to consider when deciding whether to apply for a grant:

- The restrictions placed by the funding agency on the receipt of grant funds

- The ability of the grantee organization to operate the grant program

These two elements are as important as, if not more important than, the three basics when deciding whether or not to apply for grant funding.

Funding agencies may place restrictions on their grants that dictate how a funded program is operated. For example, they may set financial terms, such as requiring matching funds and limiting what expenditures are allowed, or they may set conditions for program evaluation and reporting. They will also take into account the ability of the grantee organization to operate the grant program. These are some things you and your organization must consider:

- Do you have the necessary resources, outside of grant funds, to contribute to the project?

- Do you have the staff expertise to develop and administer the project?

- Do you have access to the proper facilities in which to conduct the project?

- Do you have the ability to sustain the project beyond the grant-funded period?

- Do you have the time and resources required to develop a cohesive, fundable proposal?

All these elements are crucial to an organization's ability to develop and write a competitive proposal, its chances of winning a grant award, and its ability to carry out a funded program. When deciding whether or not to apply for funding, you should make an *informed* decision by addressing these issues. Doing so will prevent your organization from devoting staff time and effort to developing a

proposal that will not be competitive. It will also ensure you do not win and accept a grant award when you have inadequate resources to manage the funded program or administer the grant award.

3.2 Evaluating the Advisability of a Grant Proposal

Many organizations use a rubric, a checklist, or some type of scoring system to determine whether or not the conditions are favorable to apply for a grant. The executive director and/or the board of a nonprofit organization should conduct this evaluation with the advice and counsel of program and/or grants staff *before* anyone in the organization begins writing a grant proposal. At the very least, this process will prepare the staff for the responsibilities associated with developing and writing the proposal and administering the grant, if it is awarded. Using this process should also help you avoid wasting time on a proposal that is impossible to complete by the stated deadline or that has little chance of being funded.

Use Worksheet 3 to assess the advisability of applying for a particular grant before you do the work required to complete an application.

The first three questions address the basics of determining whether or not to apply for a particular grant. If you answer no to any of the questions in Part A, you should not apply for the grant. It would be a waste of time.

The next 16 questions address a variety of issues. I suspect any organization that considers applying for a grant will have a range of answers to these questions, from yes to no to maybe. You should not base your decision to apply for a grant on your organization's ability to answer yes to each and every question. Nor should you assign a variable number of points to a yes or maybe for each question, giving some questions a higher value than others. I did not assign a point value or use another type of scoring system for this process because it would limit the critical analysis required to make the decision.

For example, I'm hesitant to say, "If you answered yes to eight or more questions, then you should proceed with the grant; if you answered no to eight or more questions, then you should not apply for the grant," because answering no to any of the questions could be a deal breaker. What matters is which questions receive a negative response, not how many. If, for example, you answered yes to question 5, but no to question 6, meaning yes, there is a match requirement and no, the organization cannot meet it, then the organization needs to evaluate its position. If it cannot meet the match requirement, then it should hold off on submitting the grant.

In another example, you may be able to answer yes to question 9, but no to question 10, meaning yes, the proposal calls for your organization to develop partnerships, but no, suitable partners have yet to be identified. This may or may not derail the submission. It is possible that your organization can go out and recruit suitable partners if time permits before an application is due.

The bottom line is that organizations should use this assessment form to get a clearer picture of what is required in a grant application prior to designing the program and writing and submitting the proposal. Modify the questions to meet the needs of your organization. Just be sure to ask the hard questions and solve any potential problems before you put time and effort into a proposal that is going nowhere!

WORKSHEET 3
GRANT PROPOSAL EFFICACY ASSESSMENT

Part A

1. Is our organization eligible to apply? _____

2. Is the size of the award adequate to fund the project? _____

3. Does the project match the funder's priorities? _____

Part B

1. Was the staff prepared for the RFP to be issued at this time? _____

2. Does the staff have the time to effectively respond to the RFP? _____

3. Does the organization currently have the staff with the necessary expertise to develop and administer the project (i.e., to serve as principal investigator or project director)?

   _____

4. Does the organization have the necessary facilities in which to conduct the project?

   _____

5. Do the grant guidelines or RFP require matching funds or other support (i.e., cash, personnel, other resources)? _____

6. Can the organization meet the match requirement? _____

7. Is long-term project funding available or necessary? _____

8. Can the institution sustain the project after the grant ends? _____

9. Are partnerships required? _____

10. Have suitable partners been identified and relationships developed?

    _____

11. Does this grant project fit in with others the institution already has in place?

    _____

12. Can the funds from this project be leveraged? _____

13. Are the requirements for evaluation and/or dissemination of the project manageable?

    _____

14. Are there any restrictions on allowable costs or activities that will hinder the project?

    _____

15. Has the organization developed a relationship with the funding agency?

    _____

16. Can the organization develop a competitive proposal? _____

3

IF YOU'RE IN THE GRANTS OFFICE, WHY AREN'T YOU WRITING THE GRANT?
PROPOSAL DEVELOPMENT AND GRANTS MANAGEMENT PROCEDURES

When I first became the coordinator of grants and contracts at Oklahoma City Community College (OCCC), I was in a constant battle with the college's faculty and staff to define my role in the grants process. Not only were my job duties misunderstood (faculty and staff regularly referred to me as the college's grant writer), but I also faced hostility from OCCC personnel seeking grant funding who came to me at the last minute with vague ideas for grants that they expected me to plan, develop, write, and submit with little or no help from them. And they fully expected these proposals to be funded! They believed I would be the program planner, decision maker, researcher, writer, and administrator for their particular grant — but all the 750 full- and part-time employees of the institution thought this!

It was not feasible for me to become an expert on TRIO programs (which provide educational opportunity for low-income and disabled Americans), disadvantaged youth, childcare, biotechnology, tutoring and mentoring, first-generation college students, technology, humanities, computer science, and so on. It was impossible for me, a single individual in an organization with 89 degree options and numerous and diverse programs, to be the institution's "grant writer." The nature of colleges and universities generally demands that they establish a single office responsible for the administrative aspects of grantsmanship, but staff in such an office rarely take on the responsibility of writing grant proposals. So what do they do instead?

1. WHAT IS THE ROLE OF THE GRANTS OFFICE?

Colleges and universities throughout the country have offices set up to deal with grants — and any college or university that doesn't have such an office should establish one! They may be called a grants office, office of grants and contracts, office of grants development, office of external funding, office of external resources, office of sponsored programs, or office of research administration — it doesn't matter; they are all the same thing. A centralized office that coordinates grant activities and provides technical assistance for grant seekers is crucial to the successful procurement of grant funding at colleges and universities.

Larger institutions, particularly universities, will have a central office of research administration or sponsored programs, but they may also have grants offices that serve the faculty of a specific college or school exclusively. For example, Oklahoma State University has a centralized office of research administration serving faculty on its campus, but the colleges of Arts and Sciences, Agricultural Sciences, and Education all have their own grants administration offices to coordinate the activities of their respective faculty, as do many of the university's other colleges.

In addition, many colleges and universities, particularly large four-year colleges and research institutions, have pre-award and post-award offices. Smaller institutions may not have separate offices, or even separate personnel, to perform these functions. It depends on the size and needs of the institution. Sample 3 contains job descriptions for a grants coordinator, pre- and post-award administrators, and a grants accountant, which give you an idea of what these jobs entail. You can use these job descriptions when you are advertising for or hiring grants personnel for your own organization.

Grants offices are generally considered to be on the academic side of the institution and therefore will report to a provost, an academic vice president, or a dean of academic affairs. They may be lumped in with offices of planning, research, or institutional effectiveness. Larger universities will have a vice president or dean of sponsored programs/research. At OCCC, the Office of Grants and Contracts is under the authority of the executive director of institutional advancement, who also happens to be the executive director of the college's foundation. Again, these arrangements vary according to an institution's size, type, and needs. As the Director of Sponsored Programs at Langston University, I report to the Vice President of Institutional Advancement and Development.

More important than the location and structure of the office or the job titles held by its personnel are the functions that the office performs. A college or university grants office should be a centralized site where faculty and staff can benefit from the expertise of grants personnel, who coordinate the grants activities of the institution. The office is responsible for procuring and managing external funding in support of institutional priorities. It organizes the proposal development process from its initial stage as an idea to final submission. Grants office personnel ensure that grant proposals adhere to institutional rules and regulations, as well as the guidelines of the funding source. The grants office ensures that the integrity of the institution is maintained.

Entrepreneurial grant seeking by the institution's faculty and staff occurs in the vacuum created when such an office does not exist. The result is confusion and a lack of communication about grants throughout the organization. In such a situation, faculty and staff may not adhere to institutional policies concerning grants and may fail to comply with funder guidelines. They may not relay information properly to administrators, other faculty, or staff, resulting in a lack of administrative support for grant projects and a lack of awareness about what projects are taking place on the campus. Internal competition occurs frequently in these situations, with two or more people from the institution responding to the same RFP or soliciting the same funder, an obvious result of not talking to one another.

SAMPLE 3
GRANTS OFFICE JOB DESCRIPTIONS

COORDINATOR OF INSTITUTIONAL GRANTS

- Works collaboratively with institution staff to identify external funding opportunities that align with the organization's vision and strategic plan and to pursue grant support for initiatives.
- Provides leadership to staff in planning and writing grant proposals.
- Researches funding opportunities available through local, state, and federal government agencies, as well as private and corporate foundations.
- Disseminates information on funding opportunities to staff.
- Reads and interprets requests for proposals and funding guidelines from government agencies and foundations to determine whether they are appropriate for the organization.
- Develops and writes grant proposals.
- Coordinates organizational meetings with staff to discuss guidelines, generate ideas, design projects, and assist in writing sections of the proposal.
- Edits and prepares proposals written by other staff for submission.
- Develops outlines, timelines, staffing plans, and budgets for grant proposals according to funding guidelines.
- Provides technical assistance to agency staff in the area of grant writing and development.
- Acts as a liaison between the institution and funding sources.
- Assists in developing and maintaining policy guidelines and budget management procedures with respect to grants awarded to the organization.
- Advises staff to ensure that grant funds are maximized and that funds awarded are spent in accordance with the guidelines provided by the funding source.
- Works with staff to assure that files and records of grant-funded projects are maintained.
- Assists in disseminating grant award information to staff, clients, board members, and other constituents of the organization.
- Is aware of applicable state and federal government regulations pertaining to the management of grant-funded programs and expenditure of government funds.
- Maintains necessary records, files, reports, databases, and other materials related to the institution's grants.
- Implements processes and procedures related to proposal development at the institution.

The applicant must possess strong research and writing abilities.

- Experience in grant writing or grants administration preferred.
- Bachelor's degree required, master's degree preferred.
- Minimum 5 years' experience in related field required.

GRANTS ADMINISTRATOR/SPONSORED PROGRAMS ADMINISTRATOR, PRE-AWARD

- Demonstrates knowledge of federal regulations for proposal development.

- Must be able to work under deadline pressure.

- Reviews proposals for submission to outside funding agencies for grant-supported projects.

- Is familiar with electronic proposal submission systems and database management programs.

- Oversees the grant submission process and provides guidance to faculty and staff seeking funding opportunities, preparing proposals, and asking questions about grants administration.

- Serves as a resource in all aspects of proposal preparation, including budget development and review, formatting, and adherence to all internal and external guidelines, regulatory requirements, and policies.

- Ensures subcontracts, consulting agreements, purchased services agreements, tech transfer agreements, and any other agreements are accurately developed and executed under the terms and conditions of the grant award.

- Ensures that grant reports are prepared on time and according to sponsor guidelines.

- Maintains institutional grants database and files of all proposals submitted by the institution, both funded and unfunded.

Experience in grant writing or grants administration required.

- Bachelor's degree required, master's degree preferred.

- Minimum 5 years' experience in related field required.

GRANTS ADMINISTRATOR/SPONSORED PROGRAMS ADMINISTRATOR, POST-AWARD

- Provides support to faculty and staff in sponsored program activities, including contract and subcontract preparation, negotiation, and recommendation for acceptance.

- Oversees projects to ensure compliance with sponsor and university rules.

- Responds to inquiries from Principal Investigators and the Office of Sponsored Programs Accounting concerning interpretation of the provisions of awards.

- Responds to requests from awarding agencies for information related to sponsored projects.

- Prepares paperwork and drafts correspondence for negotiation/acceptance of grant terms and conditions, modifications, extensions, and related administrative matters.

- Assists with the preparation and/or submission of project reports unrelated to fiscal matters of the grant award.

- Reviews and updates information pertaining to changes made to federal regulations, specific agency requirements, and procedures for administration of funded awards.

Experience in any combination of the following is preferred: procurement (federal, state, or industrial), proposal submissions, contract negotiations, grant and contract administration, and/or financial administration.

- Bachelor's degree required.

- Minimum 3 years' experience in related field required.

GRANTS ACCOUNTANT/SPONSORED PROGRAMS ACCOUNTANT, POST-AWARD

- Serves as post-award financial coordinator responsible for assuring compliance with regulations and internal control systems applicable to sponsored programs on campus.

- Provides financial technical support to faculty and staff receiving sponsored agreements.

- Performs data recording, record-keeping operations, and routine accounting for sponsored programs.

- Responsible for setting up accounting systems, designing spreadsheets, and generating financial reports of sponsored program activity.

- Assures compliance to terms and conditions of monetary awards according to OMB Circulars A-21 and A-133.

Experience with contract management, grants administration, or audit of sponsored programs in college/university, private sector, or federal government preferred.

- Bachelor's degree required.

- Minimum 12 months' experience in related field required.

The primary goal of the grants office is to control and oversee the institution's grant-seeking activities, thereby ending the confusion. Typical services provided by such an office can be divided into pre-award and post-award activities and may include the following duties:

Pre-award

- Researching funding sources

- Planning and designing programs

- Developing proposals

- Writing and editing proposals

- Producing and transmitting proposals

- Interpreting and ensuring adherence to rules, regulations, statutes, and guidelines of funding sources

Post-award

- Negotiating with funding sources

- Troubleshooting and solving problems for project directors

- Managing grant funds

- Writing and editing reports

I cannot stress enough the importance of this office to the successful development of grant proposals at organizations of all types. Institutions with successfully funded grant programs usually have functioning and effective grants offices or well-established grants processes.

2. ESTABLISHING PROCEDURES FOR PROPOSAL DEVELOPMENT AT YOUR ORGANIZATION

Now that I have described what a grants office should do, let's look at how it carries out its duties. All organizations, not just colleges and universities, will benefit from establishing the following basic procedures for developing grant proposals:

- A procedure for employees to inform the grants office of interest in, or intent to apply for, funding

- A procedure for employees to inform the organization's administrative officials about proposals being developed and to obtain approval to submit proposals

- A procedure for employees to obtain the assistance of grants personnel in the early stages of proposal planning and development, as well as a review process to ensure compliance with internal and external rules and regulations after the proposal has been completed and before it is submitted to the funding source

- A procedure for employees to obtain the signature of the organization's executive director, president, or chief executive officer prior to submitting the proposal

By establishing organizational procedures to address these four areas of concern, you will ensure that your organization provides the appropriate amount of technical assistance to grant-seeking employees, combined with the appropriate amount of administrative oversight. Depending on the size and specific needs of your organization, there may be other areas you can address using your grants procedures.

Organizations approach proposal development in one of two ways — from the bottom up, with employees suggesting grant proposals, or from the top down, with administrators controlling what grants are applied for.

All proposals start off as ideas — they might be sparked by an identified institutional or client need or in response to an RFP. In the bottom-up approach, any of an organization's employees may become grant seekers, inspired to write a grant proposal because of a particular need they identify within the organization, usually in their own area of expertise, or because an RFP comes along that suggests an idea for a proposal. This bottom-up approach is organic and grassroots in nature. However, it is also more random, difficult to monitor, and less easy to control. As a result, the bottom-up approach to developing grant proposals requires that organizations have procedures in place or chaos will ensue.

The top-down approach is used in organizations where the upper levels of the administration tightly control which proposals are developed and submitted to funding agencies. This, too, requires that established grants procedures be in place. There are usually detailed rules and a process to determine which grants the organization will apply for in a given year. Other opportunities that arise, even if they seem like good ideas, are rarely pursued. (Those unexpected opportunities that are pursued have been heavily scrutinized to determine the potential benefits to the organization and its clients.) In the top-down approach, grants development is much less random and much more strategic in nature. Grant proposals are cultivated in relationship to the institution's strategic plan. Specific funding sources and RFPs are targeted, and proposals are aligned with the organization's goals and objectives. This requires a great deal more organization.

2.1 Establishing a Proposal Development Process at Oklahoma City Community College (OCCC)

When I started work at OCCC, the college had grants procedures, but they were not routinely followed. The spirit of entrepreneurial grant seeking was alive and well on campus. Ideas were being generated, grants were being written, and proposals were being sent out at a feverish pace, with no checks and balances and no systematic plan.

Employees did not realize it wasn't a good idea to indiscriminately send out grant proposals without notifying their supervisors, not to mention college administrators, of their activities. The joke was that the janitor could write, sign, and send out a proposal without anyone batting an eye. There was no quality control. Some of the ideas were inappropriate for OCCC and did not fit into its stated mission. Other proposals were poorly written. Most never made it to an authorized official for signing; they were simply signed by lower-level employees and sent on their way.

Many of the faculty and staff writing these grants ignored funder guidelines or federal rules and regulations. Some committed college resources as matching funds without knowing whether it was feasible and without having the authority to do so. Thank goodness, most of these grants were not funded!

This had to stop. The grants office needed to be professionalized, and I was the one to do it. After seven months of trying to corral renegade faculty and staff grant writers, I decided that we needed a change in the rules. I approached my boss, who had been dealing with this problem a lot longer than I had. We were both frustrated with my lack of progress, so she agreed that I should not only update the college's grants management procedures, but also strengthen them.

I took a copy of the old rules and began to update them. It didn't take me long. I covered what I thought were all the necessary areas and then submitted the proposed changes to my boss. She looked them over and was in full agreement. We were both very excited. Things

were going to change around here — or so we thought.

Before the new grants procedures could take effect, we needed to obtain the consent of the president's cabinet, a group of vice presidents and senior administrators representing all areas of the college. When my boss, herself a member of the president's cabinet, took the proposed changes before her peers, a great deal of discussion ensued. Many of the members of the president's cabinet were not receptive to the proposed changes. She stated her case, and reluctantly they agreed to update the procedures. Over the next two sessions, the "powers that be" of the president's cabinet gutted my document, watered down my rules, and, in essence, completely missed the point of establishing grants development rules and procedures. My boss returned the new grants management procedures to my office. Funny, it looked just like the old one.

Over the next three years I dutifully followed the updated grants management procedures. The problem was that no one else at OCCC seemed to be following them. I was constantly running around, putting out fires caused by faculty and staff who refused to follow the rules. There was still a complete lack of communication between grant seekers and my office. I discovered that grants were still being submitted to funding sources without my knowledge when a foundation rejected a proposal that had been properly submitted through the grants office. The proposal was rejected, the foundation told me, because OCCC had already submitted a grant to it during the current funding cycle … no doubt the handiwork of one of the college's renegade grant writers.

Contracts for funded proposals would arrive in the president's office in need of his signature. When the office contacted me for details of the award before signing the contract, it would be the first time I had heard of the proposal, and I would have to spend the next few days tracking down the outlaw grant writer, obtaining and reviewing a copy of the proposal, and often discovering a litany of problems, such as a commitment for a cash match with no college funding source identified; a commitment for space to run a program with no campus location identified or available; commitments of faculty and/or staff time that exceeded what was allowable under federal law; statements of assurance signed by employees with no legal authority to do so; salaries budgeted that exceeded OCCC's salary scale for comparable positions; and many others.

The process clearly wasn't working. I had to institute some new rules and they had to be effective. But there was no point in drawing up more rules for my boss to present to the president's cabinet for gutting. We had to do more than simply make the administrators aware of the problem again. We needed to gain some support.

First, my boss took the college president to lunch and pleaded our case. We also had to get members of the president's cabinet on board. We sought out three vice presidents from the cabinet whose faculty and staff were the biggest offenders and responsible for some of the largest missteps concerning proposal development that I had encountered. I wanted these three on my side.

In Chapter 8 I document eight scenarios, some of which happened at OCCC, that teach 12 valuable lessons for grant seekers. I described these very scenarios to the vice presidents. I let them know what happened, who the problem employee was, and why it caused

a problem. I named names, though I told them it was not to "tattle" on their employees as much as it was to demonstrate the pervasive nature of the problem throughout their departments, throughout other departments, and at all levels of the college's hierarchy.

This strategy worked. It became obvious to them that not only was our current approach not providing a maximum benefit to OCCC in terms of securing grant funding, but it was also putting the college at risk because of the overall lack of administrative knowledge about some of the grant proposals that employees were sending out. Grant writers' failure to comply with funder regulations was another danger, particularly when federal grant funding, as well as the threat of program audits, was involved.

I contacted the college's offices of finance and human resources to get their input on the proposed rules and asked them to contact their respective presidents' cabinet members and request their support in pushing through new rules. All of the lobbying paid off, and the new grants management procedures were passed with few changes.

One of the things I learned during my tenure at the college is that change is slow. I was working in an institution that had little experience in institutional grants management. In order to make the desired changes, I had to find a few allies and point out the potential pitfalls if we did not make changes to our current way of operating. At that point, OCCC was a mere 30 years old, and grants had not been an institutional priority. There was a relaxed culture there. But this "small college" mentality had to change. We had to recognize that the college, which opened in 1972 with an enrollment of 1,049 students, now had an annual enrollment of 19,000 students and had served 28,000 when you included the individuals who participate in the college's other programs each year. Because OCCC is as large as it is, the lack of an organized grants process meant missed opportunities, wasted or duplicated efforts, and damage, potential and actual, to the college's reputation (due to misinterpreted or ignored guidelines and multiple grant submissions), among other problems.

2.2 Grants Management Procedures

After instituting the new grants procedures, I thought of the grants office as OCCC's clearinghouse for information on institutional grant activities, notices of grant opportunities, and technical assistance on foundation and government rules and regulations. It served as the official office of record, where files on all the college's grant proposals, both funded and unfunded, were maintained. I helped to organize the grants efforts of the college's faculty and staff, which made the process run more smoothly.

A centralized grants office with a methodical approach to developing grant proposals is the only logical way for a large organization to manage its grants activities. Establishing policies and procedures and consistently abiding by the rules will help any organization, large or small, maintain order and effectively compete for funding.

At the end of this chapter, I've included examples of some of the rules and forms I developed for OCCC, including the Grants Management Procedures (Sample 4), a flowchart detailing the process for proposal completion (Figure 1), the Grant Registration and Approval Form (Worksheet 4), and a timeline for grant application (Sample 5). Any organization, no matter the size or type, can implement similar procedures. I encourage you to use the OCCC examples as a starting point for

developing your own grants management process and customize them to the needs of your particular organization.

3. GRANTS DEVELOPMENT IN A SMALL NONPROFIT ORGANIZATION

A nonprofit organization, or single-issue agency, is driven by a narrowly defined mission and provides services to a specific constituency. Small nonprofits often do not have the resources to hire a full-time grant writer. They may have someone on staff who combines grant writing with other duties to help carry out the organizational mission. That one person may be the event planner, coordinator of direct-mail appeals, director of planned giving efforts, organizer of the capital campaign, and grant writer extraordinaire!

The first rule of writing proposals for a small, nonprofit organization is to thoroughly understand the organization's constituency. The grant writer must have extensive knowledge of the organization's mission, the services it provides, and the clientele it serves, because he or she is often designing the program for which the grant proposal is being written, as well as writing the proposal.

Regardless of who writes the grant proposals in a small, nonprofit organization, it is essential that you establish either a formal grants office or a simple grants process. If grant writing is one of several hats that you wear at your organization, your "grants office" may consist of a couple of file drawers. If your only job is to write grants, you should commit a greater amount of time and effort to setting up the office and establishing an organizational grants process.

It's easy to control the process when you are the sole individual responsible for writing and submitting grant proposals. If more than one person at the organization writes the proposals, it is important that the lines of communication are open. It's best to have one person who serves as the single point of contact for coordinating the organization's grant activities. If this is not possible, set up a shared database or use another method that gives all employees access to the organization's grants information.

Just as it is for a university or college, the purpose of the grants office and any grants management procedures is to ensure a smooth process for your organization's grant-seeking efforts, adherence to funder rules and regulations, and successful procurement and administration of grant funding. Small non-profits should keep the following points in mind when establishing a proposal development process:

- *Avoid duplication of efforts.* It is not uncommon for two or more people at an organization to write separate grants to the same funder, especially foundations. This happens when there is no organized process for coordinating who will write which grants. Such a process is vital, even in small organizations.

- *Build review into the process.* Require that grant proposals, especially those for federal government grants, be reviewed by a fresh pair of eyes within the organization before you submit them. The person writing the grant proposal is not always the best person to ensure that it is in full compliance with funder rules and regulations.

- *Control the quality of proposals that your organization submits.* The person who wrote the grant proposal will have worked on it day in and day out over a

long period of time and will be so familiar with the document that he or she will miss errors, ignore poor writing, and fail to objectively evaluate its overall cohesiveness. This is another reason for a second person to step in to help before the proposal is submitted.

- *Make sure people are aware of what grants you are applying for.* It's important for the organization's executive director and/or governing board to be aware of what grants are being applied for. First of all, grant writers must obtain the proper authority to submit proposals, and it's likely the executive director's or president's signature will be required on the proposal. It's also possible that members of the governing board may be called upon to endorse a particular program or to put in a good word for the organization with the program officers and/or members of the governing boards of funding agencies.

- *Determine your financial and administrative responsibilities.* Find out what financial and administrative oversight you must give to funded proposals. This process should be coordinated, diligently monitored, and accurately documented. It is essential if you want to gain the trust of funders, establish your organization's credibility, and attract more grant dollars to your programs.

4. GRANTS DEVELOPMENT AT FAITH-BASED ORGANIZATIONS

Grants development at a faith-based organization operates in much the same way as it does at a small nonprofit organization. Faith-based organizations generally engage in social service activities and may receive grant funding from a variety of federal agencies to run public social service programs.

On January 29, 2001, US President George W. Bush issued an executive order creating the White House Office of Faith-Based and Community Initiatives (now the White House Office of Faith-Based and Neighborhood Partnerships). The purpose of the office is to identify and eliminate barriers that faith-based and community organizations encounter when they seek federal grant funding. The office also provides technical assistance on grantsmanship to those organizations.

Contrary to popular belief, it was not unlawful for faith-based organizations to apply for and receive federal grant funding before this office was created. The Salvation Army and Catholic Charities are examples of faith-based organizations with national and international reputations that have provided social services to the public for many years and sometimes receive federal funding to do so. However, the Office of Faith-Based and Community Initiatives has made it easier than ever for such organizations, which are often small, to seek out and receive grant funding.

Faith-based organizations are similar to other small nonprofit organizations in that they lack knowledge of and experience in navigating the world of grants. They are unlike other nonprofit organizations, however, because they must separate their regular religious activities from their secular social services activities when receiving grant funding. The United States Supreme Court has declared that direct government support cannot be used by faith-based organizations for "inherently religious" activities. This means that faith-based organizations cannot use federal grant funds to promote religious worship,

instruction, or proselytization. They cannot require individuals to participate in religious activities or practices in order to take advantage of federally funded programs, nor can they use religious-themed materials in federally funded programs.

Under the Internal Revenue Service code, churches are automatically tax-exempt by virtue of being religious organizations. However, many churches and other religious organizations seek out 501(c)(3) status in order to ensure that contributors' donations are tax-deductible. Many also establish separate 501(c)(3) organizations to receive grant funding, which makes it easier to distinguish between secular grant-funded activities and their religious operations.

If you are developing a grants management process for a religious organization, you'll want to establish rules similar to those that apply to colleges and universities, as well as small nonprofit organizations. Whether the faith-based organization is large or small, it should put the following procedures in place:

- Ensure there is at least one dedicated staff member who is responsible for organizing and maintaining all grant files and documentation.

- Establish a process for the organization's executive director (who may also be the minister, pastor, or other church leader) to review the proposal.

- Establish a process for the church board or separate nonprofit board to review the proposal.

- Establish a signature process for all proposals submitted.

- Keep religious and secular activities separate, and ensure that all staff know and understand federal regulations, by providing training to those staff delivering grant-funded programs.

- Monitor grant-funded programs to fulfill administrative and financial requirements.

5. WHAT IS THE ROLE OF THE GRANT WRITER?

The role of the grant writer is to write the grant, of course. This is a no-brainer, right?

Well, yes and no. The role of the grant writer varies by organization. The type of organization you work for determines the duties of the position, as well as the job title. Most grant writers in their pure form are regular employees of a single-issue agency, and their most basic duty is to develop and write grant proposals. This type of grant writer familiarizes himself or herself with the agency's mission and writes grants in support of this mission. He or she becomes an expert on the agency's single issue and its programs. For example, grant writers working for the American Lung Association write grant proposals for programs geared toward fighting lung cancer and other lung diseases, putting an end to smoking, etc. These grant writers will know everything about lung diseases and smoking because it is nearly impossible to do a credible job selling a program in a grant proposal if you know nothing about it (see Sample 6 at the end of this chapter for a description of a grant writer's job).

In some organizations, the grant writer is the project director or program manager. This individual is responsible for developing grant proposals in his or her area and for writing most, if not all, of the grant proposals. For example, the director of the Head Start Program at the (fictitious) Dodge City Youth and Family Services writes grant proposals in support of daycare, early childhood education, and preschool programming. These grants support the agency's Head Start Program.

However, in another scenario, Dodge City Youth and Family Services might employ a grant writer on its staff. This person not only develops and writes grants to support the Head Start Program, but he or she also prepares grants to support the agency's Youthful Offender Program, Homeless and Runaway Youth Program, Drug and Alcohol Prevention Program, and others. As the agency's grant writer, this individual must have some knowledge of the agency's various programs, but he or she develops and writes grant proposals in conjunction with the program directors and engages program personnel in the process of developing the proposals' content, so he or she does not have to be as familiar with the program as the writer in the first scenario.

 Grant writing does not take place in a vacuum. If you are the lone grant writer at your organization, consider forming grant-writing teams. This is especially helpful for writing and completing federal grant proposals, simply because of their complexity and length. Also, because the grant writer is not likely to be the project director, it is helpful to have the project design and the proposal influenced by the "experts."

In a third scenario, the "grant writer" at Dodge City Youth and Family Services might actually function as a grants administrator. He or she assists program managers and other program staff as they develop and write proposals, but the grants administrator's main role is to manage or coordinate grants activity throughout the organization. He or she is responsible for maintaining the grants office, tracking grants activity, maintaining files of proposals submitted, providing technical assistance to the agency's grant seekers, serving as liaison between the agency and funders at all levels, ensuring that grant proposals adhere to internal and funder rules and regulations, and monitoring funded programs.

In an academic setting, grant writing fulfills the criteria for participation in scholarly activity that many institutions require when they are considering faculty for promotion and tenure. Grant writing is akin to research and publishing in one's field, particularly in the four-year university system. Because of this, faculty members are expected to write their own grants. It's a natural outgrowth of scholarship.

6. WHEN GRANTS OFFICE PERSONNEL BECOME PROJECT DIRECTORS

People who do not grasp the full scope of the grantsmanship process often misunderstand the role of the grants administrator. They look upon all grants office personnel as "grant writers" in simple terms — the one who writes the grants — not understanding that program staff must provide much of the information that goes into the grant proposals, or at least help in the proposal's initial development.

This lack of understanding often becomes a misperception that the writing of the grant proposal is the beginning and the end of the process; in reality, it's neither. Grant seekers must conduct research to find a funder, interpret an RFP, gain approval from the authorized organizational representative(s) to

submit the proposal, develop a concept, conduct more research to support the proposal, and write and submit the proposal. Grants office personnel provide the technical assistance to accomplish those tasks and more. If the proposal is funded, grants office personnel play an integral role in contract negotiation, financial and programmatic monitoring, and reporting, working hand-in-hand with project directors, but not themselves becoming the project director.

If their roles are not clearly defined, grants office personnel may find themselves taking on the role of project director for newly funded projects. I caution against this. In some organizations this setup works, but there are many situations where it doesn't:

- *The larger the organization, the less likely it is to work.* Presumably a large organization hires a grants administrator because there are enough grant proposals being developed and written, and there are enough existing grant-funded programs, to keep him or her busy providing technical assistance to grant seekers and administrative oversight for funded programs. However, if the grants administrator also takes on the position of project director of XYZ grant-funded program, he or she will be less able to provide assistance and oversight.

- *The more diverse the programming, the less likely it is to work.* The more diverse the organization's programming, the less likely it is that one individual will be qualified to manage the day-to-day operations of XYZ grant-funded program, let alone oversee many different grant-funded programs. For most large grants, federal grants in particular, the job of project director is a full-time grant-funded position.

- *The more grant-funded programs the organization has, the less likely it is to work.* See the previous explanation.

- *The smaller the staff of the grants office, the less likely it is to work.* If the grants office has a small staff (many are one-person operations), how feasible is it for one person to provide micro-level, hands-on management for one program in addition to the macro-level oversight of several grant-funded programs, not to mention the primary role he or she must play in proposal development and submission?

It is rare for colleges, universities, research institutions, and teaching hospitals to blur the duties of grant writers, program directors, and grants administrators, as organizations with more loosely constructed grants offices and processes might do. Partly, this is because large institutions possess three of the four characteristics that I warned would make it difficult to merge the grant writer/grants administrator role with that of the project director/program manager.

First, large colleges, universities, research institutions, and teaching hospitals are more likely than smaller organizations to have a purely administrative "Office of Sponsored Programs" or "Office of Research Administration." (These are two common academic terms for grants offices that perform administrative functions only. The terms are rarely used outside the field of academia or research.)

Second, purely administrative offices of sponsored programs/research administration are more likely to be found in organizations with a significant amount of diverse programming.

Third, these offices are more likely to be found in organizations that submit a large number of grant proposals and possess a significant amount of grant-funded programming that requires management and oversight. This type of institution must have a rigid organizational and procedural method for developing and submitting grant proposals and administering and managing funded projects.

Finally, it is obvious, but still important to note, that colleges, universities, research institutions, and teaching hospitals conduct most of the grant-funded technical and scientific research in this country. It's not likely a grant writer would be able to write a fundable proposal in any number of these technical and scientific disciplines, even if he or she possessed training in a technical field; nor would grants office personnel be qualified to serve as project directors on such projects. However, it is also important to note that grants office personnel in these settings provide an invaluable service to Principal Investigators and project directors who write their own grants but need the expertise of grants administrators to survive in the often complicated world of adhering to funder guidelines in proposal preparation and submission, understanding and fulfilling contractual obligations, reporting, deciphering rules and regulations, and interpreting the language of grantsmanship. For more on the roles of project personnel in writing the grant, refer to section **5.4** in Chapter 4.

SAMPLE 4
GRANTS MANAGEMENT PROCEDURES

1. The process for initiating a grant proposal at Oklahoma City Community College is the same, regardless of whether the grant is being submitted through the College or through the Oklahoma City Community College Foundation on behalf of a College program.

2. Before an employee of Oklahoma City Community College initiates a grant proposal of any kind, regardless of the dollar amount being requested, he or she must contact the Office of Grants and Contracts and complete a Grant Registration and Approval Form. This form must be completed for all requests to organizations outside of the College to fund projects, requires the signed approval of the employee's direct supervisor and his or her respective President's Cabinet member, and must be promptly returned to the Office of Grants and Contracts.

3. Upon receipt of the Grant Registration and Approval Form, the Coordinator of Grants and Contracts will establish a timeline to be utilized by Project Directors and Principal Investigators to facilitate proposal completion.

4. President's Cabinet must approve all grant requests of $25,000 or more. President's Cabinet must also approve grant proposals requiring a cash or in-kind College resources. Under these circumstances, the Grant Registration and Approval Form must be presented by the employee's President's Cabinet member for review by the full Cabinet. This form should be presented to President's Cabinet no less than 30 days prior to the grant's due date, unless other arrangements are made with the Coordinator of Grants and Contracts. The Grant Registration and Approval Form must be returned to the Office of Grants and Contracts within 3 days of being approved or declined by President's Cabinet.

5. Information regarding grant personnel must be established once the Grant Registration and Approval Form is approved by President's Cabinet. The Project Director will work with Human Resources to develop a detailed job description where required, establish salary level, and calculate benefits. Human Resources will review personnel information in the completed proposal before submission.

6. The consent of the President and/or President's Cabinet must be received before any department or program in the College may enter into a Memorandum of Agreement with another institution for grant purposes on behalf of the College as a whole. Letters of support to other organizations for the purposes of being used in another's grant proposal do not require consent of the President's Cabinet.

7. Final drafts of completed proposals must be sent to the Office of Grants and Contracts for review one week prior to the proposal or mailing deadline. During this time, the Coordinator of Grants and Contracts will review the completed proposal and ensure that the project complies with internal and external requirements; and the Office of Finance will review the grant proposal budget for compliance and accuracy. The Coordinator of Grants and Contracts will obtain the required signature from the College's authorized signing authority. After all approvals and signatures are obtained, the Coordinator of Grants and Contracts duplicates, packages, and ships the proposal to the funding agency.

Reprinted with permission of the Offices of Institutional Advancement and Grants and Contracts, Oklahoma City Community College.

SELF-COUNSEL PRESS/GETTING GRANTS/06

8. The President of the College, the Executive Director of Institutional Advancement, and the Provost/Vice President for Academic Affairs are the only authorized organizational representatives at Oklahoma City Community College permitted to sign grant applications. There may be grants that require signatures from Project Directors/Principal Investigators in addition to the authorized signature.

9. The Office of Grants and Contracts is the designated authorized institutional representative for all electronic/Internet-based proposal maintenance and submission.

10. Project Directors and Principal Investigators are required to forward copies of documents such as award letters, denial letters, major budget changes, reports, and other important documents related to the College's grant proposals to the Office of Grants and Contracts.

11. Failure to adhere to any of the rules governing the grants management process at Oklahoma City Community College may result in a proposal not being approved for submission or a funded project not being accepted.

FIGURE 1
PROCESS FOR PROPOSAL COMPLETION

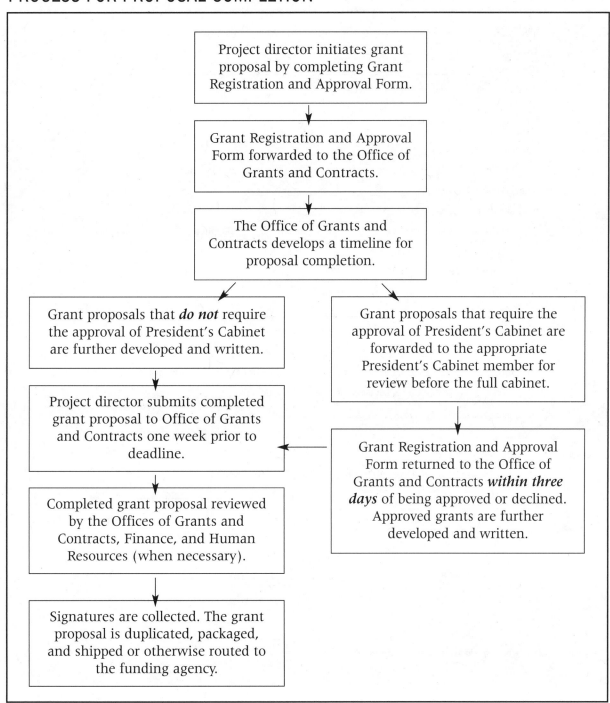

Project director initiates grant proposal by completing Grant Registration and Approval Form.

Grant Registration and Approval Form forwarded to the Office of Grants and Contracts.

The Office of Grants and Contracts develops a timeline for proposal completion.

Grant proposals that *do not* require the approval of President's Cabinet are further developed and written.

Grant proposals that require the approval of President's Cabinet are forwarded to the appropriate President's Cabinet member for review before the full cabinet.

Project director submits completed grant proposal to Office of Grants and Contracts one week prior to deadline.

Grant Registration and Approval Form returned to the Office of Grants and Contracts *within three days* of being approved or declined. Approved grants are further developed and written.

Completed grant proposal reviewed by the Offices of Grants and Contracts, Finance, and Human Resources (when necessary).

Signatures are collected. The grant proposal is duplicated, packaged, and shipped or otherwise routed to the funding agency.

WORKSHEET 4
GRANT REGISTRATION AND APPROVAL FORM

Employee initiating request: _____

Title: _____

Department: _____

Reviewed by Office of Grants and Contracts: _____

Project name: _____

Funding agency: _____

Amount being requested: _____

Match requirement: _____ None _____ Cash _____ In-kind   Amount: _____

Source(s) of cash match: _____

In-kind college resources required:

_____ Personnel _____ Facilities _____ Equipment _____ Supplies _____Photocopying

_____ Vehicles _____ Other: _____

Will any new positions be created? _____ Yes _____ No   If so, how many? _____

Will additional space be required to house this project? _____ Yes _____ No

If so, how much? _____

Duration of project: _____ One-time grant _____ Multiyear grant

Length of project: _____ · Start/End dates: _____

Does this project require the College to enter into a Consortium or Partnership Agreement?

_____ Yes _____ No   If so, list the partnering organization(s): _____

_____

_____

Deadline for submission: _____

What College priority (end statement) will this project help to accomplish?

_____

_____

Population served by this project: _____

_____

Brief project description: _____

_____

_____

_____

Reprinted with permission of the Office of Grants and Contracts, Oklahoma City Community College.

SELF-COUNSEL PRESS/GETTING GRANTS/06

WORKSHEET 4 — CONTINUED

Signatures required for grant submission or consideration by President's Cabinet:

_____   _____
Employee Initiating Grant Request   Department Head/Chair

_____   _____
Dean (if appropriate)   President's Cabinet Member

To be completed by President's Cabinet ONLY when President's Cabinet approval required for grant submission:

Does this project fit within the College's mission and strategic plan? _____ Yes _____ No

Does the Project Director have adequate information to respond to the RFP and sufficient time to develop a competitive proposal before the deadline date? _____ Yes _____ No

Is the College willing and able to commit the necessary resources (e.g., space, personnel, matching funds) to support the project? _____ Yes _____ No

_____ **Approved**   _____ **Denied**   **Date:** _____

SAMPLE 5
TIMELINE FOR XYZ GRANT APPLICATION

Activity	Parties Responsible	Deadline Date
Grant Registration and Approval Form presented at President's Cabinet Meeting	Provost/Vice President for Academic Affairs	No later than November 1, 2009
Email the completed grant proposal containing the following items to the Office of Grants and Contracts: • 50–70 page proposal narrative • Budget in format specified by RFP • Budget narrative	Dean of Math and Science or other designated Math and Science faculty	Noon, December 1, 2009
Review completed proposal; Gather required attachments; Complete certifications and assurances	Office of Grants and Contracts	December 1–4, 2009
Review budget	Office of Finance	December 1–4, 2009
Review personnel information	Office of Human Resources	December 1–4, 2009
Obtain signature of Project Director/Principal Investigator	Office of Grants and Contracts	December 4–5, 2009
Obtain signature of President, Provost, or Executive Director of Institutional Advancement	Office of Grants and Contracts	December 4–6, 2009
Prepare proposal package; Make and distribute copies of completed proposal; Mail, hand deliver, or otherwise route proposal package to funding agency	Office of Grants and Contracts	December 7, 2009

Signatures Required for Grant Submission:

_____

Office of Finance

_____

Office of Human Resources

_____

Office of Grants and Contracts

SAMPLE 6
GRANT WRITER JOB DESCRIPTION

Organization seeks a creative thinker with the ability to articulate the vision and mission of the organization.

Responsibilities of this position include:

- Researching grant sources.
- Writing proposals.
- Tracking and submitting financial reports as needed.
- Compiling and submitting final reports to funders.

Applicant must possess strong research and writing abilities:

- Experience in technical writing or grant writing preferred.
- Bachelor's degree required.
- Minimum 6 to 12 months' experience in related field preferred.

YOU EXPECT ME *TO WRITE IT?*
WRITING THE GRANT PROPOSAL

This chapter is devoted to the actual mechanical aspects of grant writing. Now that you've done the research, found grants to apply for, and assessed your organization's ability to complete a competitive proposal, it's time to discuss what your proposal should look like. The first thing to remember when beginning to write a grant proposal is: Don't panic. It looks a lot more intimidating than it actually is, particularly if you are staring down at a federal application package that's about an inch thick! Break down each part of the proposal into smaller sections and write one section at a time. You don't even have to write the sections in order. I rarely do. Start with the section that comes easiest to you.

The material you are expected to cover will vary from funder to funder. There is some standardization across federal grant programs and agencies. For example, different agencies use some of the same grant forms (i.e., cover page, budget page, etc.), and many programs within the same agency will require standardized content and formatting. Not only do many of the grant programs within the US Department of Education use the same forms, but the formatting requirements and section headings are also identical in many of its grants.

When it comes to foundation and corporate grants, though, there is little standardization because each organization is self-contained. Each sets up and operates its own individual grant programs. Some foundations have come together in regional associations of grant makers in an attempt to streamline and simplify the grant-making process. There are several of these groups in the United States, made up of foundations from a specific area (defined by a state or regional geographic boundary) that have standardized their rules for grant making and often use the same application format and forms, called "Common Grant Applications" or CGAs. You can find out if there is such an organization in your area by contacting the Forum of Regional Associations of Grantmakers (www.givingforum.org), accessing the Foundation Center's website, using a foundation directory, or contacting your local community foundation for information.

However, whether a grant proposal is aimed at a government agency or a private foundation or corporation, it generally contains two major parts: the **narrative section** and the **budget**. In this chapter, I outline the basic concepts you will need to address in the narrative section of a grant proposal, regardless of funder. In Chapter 5, I cover the budget. These sections may be called other names, but once you read your RFP or funder guidelines, you will be able to identify the narrative and budget section and determine what information the funder is requesting in its particular proposal.

1. LETTER OF INQUIRY/INTENT

Often foundations and corporations request that grant seekers submit a **letter of inquiry** (sometimes called a **letter of intent**) before submitting a formal proposal (see Sample 7). This is so the funders can screen out projects that do not meet their funding guidelines and avoid wasting time and energy wading through lengthy, inappropriate proposals. The funder may also want to preselect those projects in which it has an interest and then request full proposals only from the selected group of grant seekers. This can be a benefit to grant seekers, as it means they don't have to spend time and effort preparing a lengthy proposal that does not meet the funder's requirements or interest.

A letter of inquiry should be brief (no more than one to three pages). It should be written on letterhead stationery, and the body of the letter should contain the following paragraphs:

1. *Introduction:* Explain why you are writing. Introduce your organization to the funder, with information on the organization's mission and the population it serves.

2. *Project description:* Define your project. Establish a connection between the funder's priorities and the goals of your project.

3. *Needs:* Establish the need for the project. Use demographic and statistical information.

4. *Solution:* Discuss how your proposed project would address the identified need and solve the problem. Briefly review the literature and mention any best practices that support your project idea.

5. *Project plan:* Describe the project activities, methodology used, and timetable for project completion.

6. *Organizational capacity:* Discuss your organization's ability to carry out the project. Include information on previous work you've done in the program area and any demonstrated institutional commitment to the success of the project. State the qualifications of key project personnel.

7. *Budget:* State how much funding your organization will need to support the project. Break it down by requested funding, organizational funding, and funding from other sources (see Chapter 5).

8. *Sustainability:* Explain how the organization will continue the program after the grant funds are expended.

Sometimes federal, state, and local government grant competitions will require that potential applicants submit a letter of intent. Often this is a true letter of "intent," especially when it is for a federal government competition. The funding agency wants to gauge the expected response to its RFP, so it asks how

LETTER OF INQUIRY

The Youth Center
4567 ABC Road
Anywhere, OK 73456

September 1, 2009

Ms. Susan McDaniels, President
McDaniels Family Foundation
1234 XYZ Boulevard
Anywhere, OK 73123

Dear Ms. McDaniels:

On behalf of The Youth Center, I am writing to express an interest in submitting a formal application for funding from your Foundation's "Youth and Families" grant program. The Youth Center was opened in 1975 and is a 501(c)(3) nonprofit organization serving Anywhere, Oklahoma. The mission of our organization is "to offer abused, neglected, and troubled children and adolescents a safe environment in which to grow, heal, and learn." Our organization serves children and adolescents in the juvenile justice system, foster care system, and the community at large in the four-county area surrounding the city of Anywhere.

We would like to propose a project to aid runaway and troubled teens in the four-county area. The "Runaway and Troubled Teens Project" complements the focus of the McDaniels Family Foundation, as demonstrated by the funding guidelines of your "Youth and Families" grant initiative. The focus of your program on assisting troubled youth develop life skills, promote citizenship, and address underlying problems of concern in the home fits the focus of The Youth Center's project.

According to a Spring 2008 publication of the Council on Troubled Teens, the number of teenagers running away from home and ending up in the juvenile justice or foster care systems in the state of Oklahoma increased by 11 percent between 2006 and 2007. Data collected by The Youth Center on teenage runaways in the previous three fiscal years verify the phenomenon. The number of teenagers living in the four-county area reported to have "run away" from home in calendar year 2007 was 1,640. This is an increase of 7 percent over calendar year 2006 in our service area alone.

The focus of the "Runaway and Troubled Teens Project" is to target youth identified in the community by parents, teachers, and the court system as "runaways," defined as out of the home for two nights in a row without parental permission. Research shows that many teens who run away from home are experiencing extreme distress and do not have the ability to cope with parents, peers, or school. Thus, they run away. Many return home, but some run away repeatedly, which increases their chances of entering the state juvenile justice and foster care systems. In fact, frequent runaways are four times more likely to end up in the state system.

According to best practices in troubled teen research, juveniles who are subjected to frequent counseling, both personal and group, combined with training that develops coping skills and anger-management training, have a chance to break the cycle.

Our project proposes to offer intensive counseling and alternative therapies to adolescents referred to our agency. Each teenager will be evaluated upon referral and must attend counseling twice weekly (one personal counseling session, one group counseling session) over a six-month period. Therapy will focus on all aspects of adolescents' lives from family to peer groups, to school. Upon program completion, students will receive monthly follow-up services for up to one year.

The Youth Center has been serving the four-county area for 30 years. Our agency specializes in the problems of troubled children, youth, and families in our service area. We have three licensed practical counselors on staff and two marriage and family counselors. The Youth Center is certified by the National Board of Certification.

We are seeking support in the amount of $70,000 to hire a fourth licensed practical counselor ($50,000 salary and benefits) to work exclusively with program participants. $10,000 of the funds allocated to this program will be used to provide program participants with coping skills, and self-esteem incentives. The remaining $10,000 will be used for training materials, job placement assistance, and group activities.

In year two of the program, the County Commissioners of Anywhere have agreed to provide The Youth Center with up to $15,000 for services provided to 500 teens. The Center plans to seek similar agreements with the other counties in our service area.

Thank you for your consideration of our request.

Sincerely,

Marjorie Jones

Ms. Marjorie Jones, Director
(800) 123-4567

---

many organizations intend to submit a proposal. This helps the agency plan for the competition and ensure it has enough proposal readers to review the number of grants submitted. This letter of intent is usually very short, sometimes consisting of only one paragraph.

 Write, edit, rewrite, and refine!

2. ABSTRACT/EXECUTIVE SUMMARY

An **abstract**, also called a **summary** or **executive summary**, is a synopsis of your grant proposal. It is often the first page of substantial content in a proposal (after the title page and table of contents), but most of the grant writers I know don't actually write the abstract until they've finished writing the proposal — for obvious reasons. How do you accurately summarize a proposal that hasn't yet been written?

The abstract should be succinct (no more than two pages). Many federal grant programs limit applicants to a one-page abstract. It should contain the same information as a letter of inquiry:

- Introduction to the organization

- Project description

- Description of needs
- Solution
- Project plan
- Information on organizational capacity
- Budget
- Plans for sustainability

The main difference between an abstract and a letter of inquiry is that the letter is written *before* a full proposal is developed and will likely be much more general. An abstract, written after the proposal is complete, lends itself to refinement. As a result, the abstract is accurate and concise.

Instead of writing separate paragraphs, several sentences long, for each content area, you should consolidate the paragraphs, eliminate extraneous information, and focus on each concept in one or two sentences.

1. *Introduction/Project description:* Begin the abstract by describing the project for which funding is being sought. Introduce the organization seeking funding for the project and establish its eligibility to apply. Identify the population served by the organization.

2. *Needs/Solution:* Describe the problem to be addressed. Use one or two significant statistics that demonstrate the extent of the need. Explain how the project will solve the problem it was designed to address.

3. *Project plan/Organizational capacity:* Define the project's main goals and outcomes. Briefly indicate the organization's capacity to carry out such a project, how the project will be evaluated, and any plans for dissemination.

4. *Budget/Sustainability:* Identify funds required and requested. Mention any sources of additional funding or other resources. State how the project will be sustained after funding ends.

Remember that the abstract serves as an overview of the proposal. You will not be able to restate the entire contents of the proposal on the one or two pages allowed.

3. ORGANIZATIONAL DESCRIPTION

The **organizational description** is usually one of the shorter sections of a grant proposal — whether it is for a foundation or a state or federal agency. This is where you identify and describe your organization. State the organization's full name and location, when it was established, the population it serves, the types of services it provides, the number of people it employs, and the number of "clients" it serves. Include any other information that is important, interesting, or impressive and relevant.

Because you will use this same information in all grant proposals, no matter what the funding source, save time by compiling it once and using the same text in every proposal. Update the organizational description annually and keep an electronic version on your computer and several hard copies in a file. Insert this information into your grant proposals whenever necessary.

If the grant project is a partnership or collaboration among two or more organizations, the organizational description should include a paragraph or two on each of the organizations involved.

4. NEEDS STATEMENT

The **needs statement** is the heart and soul of a grant proposal. It is not a statement in the sense of a simple one-sentence declaration. Rather, it is a detailed account of the problem or need to be addressed. Without a tight, well-written needs statement, your proposal has no merit. If you cannot demonstrate a need for whatever program or project your organization is seeking to fund, then why would anyone give you a grant for it? If you cannot justify the need, there is no point continuing with the proposal. An effective needs statement must have the following characteristics:

- It is clear and concise, specifically and pointedly identifying the need or problem to be addressed.

- It focuses on the needs of the organization's clients, constituency, or target population, not on the needs of the organization itself.

- It uses statistics to demonstrate the severity of the need.

4.1 Clearly Identify the Need

In order to create a powerful needs statement, you must be specific when you identify the problem to be addressed. Here are two examples of needs statements (note that all institutions in these examples are fictitious):

Unclear Needs Statement

The Johnsonville School District is seeking grant funding to support its program for high school dropouts. The district has found that students drop out of school due to failing grades, a lack of interest in school, and a lack of parental support.

Clear Needs Statement

The Johnsonville School District has the highest high school dropout rate in the state of Texas. The district has found that the three most common reasons students drop out of high school are failing grades, a lack of interest in school, and a lack of parental support. To combat the dropout problem, the Johnsonville School District is seeking grant funding to implement its Stay in School Program districtwide. The Stay in School Program will provide students with tutoring, mentoring, paid work experience, and out-of-school activities tied to grades. It will also provide outreach to parents of students at risk of dropping out of school.

In the first example, the funder learns that the Johnsonville School District is seeking funding to support its high school dropout prevention program. This is fine, but does it translate into an identifiable need? Is the problem stated clearly?

The second example is much better at translating the same request for funding into a clearly visible need. The first sentence sets the tone of the section and specifically identifies the problem.

4.2 Focus on Need of Target Population

When you seek funding for a grant project, your organization's need alone is never enough to justify why a grant should be awarded. Here are two examples of statements justifying the need for funding:

**Organization's Need —
Poor Justification for Funding**

The Johnsonville School District is unable to pay teachers to tutor students after school and on weekends as part of our program to address the high dropout rate in the district. We are requesting grant funding to assist us with this need.

**Target Population's Need —
Good Justification for Funding**

The Johnsonville School District has the highest high school dropout rate in the state of Texas. More than 18 percent of the district's students drop out of high school before completing 12th grade. Research shows that students who fail to complete high school are most likely to live in poverty as adults, are more likely to be convicted of criminal activity, and are more likely to suffer from substance abuse. The district has found that the three most common reasons students drop out of high school are failing grades, a lack of interest in school, and a lack of parental support. The district's Stay in School Program is designed to reduce the dropout rate by offering tutoring and mentoring, paid work experiences and out-of-school activities tied to grades, and outreach to parents of students at risk of dropping out of school. The district is seeking funding to pay teachers to tutor students after school and on weekends to support the initiative.

In the first example, the writer identifies the need as the Johnsonville School District's inability to pay teachers to tutor students after school and on weekends. Though this is a true need that exists within the district, it fails as justification for grant funding because it is only one need of one organization and is not adequately tied to a "greater need."

The second example is much better at tying the need of the district to the needs of the target population. The district's inability to pay teachers to tutor students is not just a problem of the district; it is a problem of the students at risk of dropping out of school. In this way, the need is presented as a social need, a community need. The second example effectively conveys the connection between the problem (the high-school dropout rate), the solution (tutoring and mentoring, among other alternatives), and the need (funding to pay teachers for tutoring after school and on weekends).

4.3 Use Statistics

The *judicious* use of demographic and statistical information is important if you want to write a compelling needs statement. You can find statistics everywhere and should use them to tell how many, how much, how often, how severe, how costly, etc. I emphasize "judicious" because you should use statistics but not overuse them.

Be careful when selecting the statistics you will use to demonstrate your need. Make sure that the statistical data you choose is relevant to the need being addressed. Do not use dramatic figures that paint a negative picture of an area or target population just to demonstrate how bad things are. You should tie this information directly to the problem that you are trying to solve.

The first place to go to look for statistics is the US Census Bureau (www.census.gov). If you have never visited the Census Bureau website, take the time to do so and learn how to extract information from the site. The amount of information the federal government collects through the census is staggering and can be broken down in so many ways — from national figures to state, county, city, and even zip code figures.

When using statistics, think small — or should I say local? Grant proposals are usually written for a small, local, target population. If you are writing a grant on homelessness in your city, it is more useful to get the city's statistics on homelessness rather than figures on homelessness across the United States. State and national figures are useful for making comparisons, but you should not use them exclusively to justify why your city needs to build a new homeless shelter. To make such a case, you will need to obtain local statistics on the problem.

There are many other options available to grant seekers looking for statistical information to support grant proposals. The website of the US Department of Labor's Bureau of Labor Statistics (www.bls.gov) offers a variety of employment and economic data, and many other federal, state, and local government agencies collect statistics on diverse issues. Public school districts, colleges, and universities often have offices of research and planning that collect and publish data on demographic and statistical trends affecting their organizations and the populations they serve.

State and local sources of information are often more effective and reliable than federal census information because they are more recent. Try to cite the most up-to-date statistics in your grant proposals. If possible, do not use information that is more than three years old.

 Maintain a file of information to support the needs statements of all your grant proposals. Include items such as statistical data, reports, newspaper articles, white papers, and any other pertinent information that you come across during the year. When it's time to write your proposal, you will not have to conduct research to support the needs of your program or population.

Another excellent source of statistics is local nonprofits and associations. These organizations often collect data from their target population every day, and this data can provide the most compelling proof to demonstrate need to a funder. For example, the volunteer members of a church in my community prepared and delivered 250 meals per week to 50 elderly residents in the neighborhood. The church applied to a local funder for a grant to support the meals program. The most compelling data it provided to demonstrate need was the waiting list it had compiled in the previous six months: the church had been contacted by an additional 130 elderly citizens or their families seeking assistance/meals from the church's program. Serving an additional 130 residents would increase the number of meals prepared each week from 250 to 900! The church cited those numbers in the grant proposal and powerfully communicated the community's need to the funder. (By the way, the grant was funded.)

Here are two examples of paragraphs presenting statistical information:

Lacking Statistical Information to Emphasize Need

The Johnsonville School District has the highest high school dropout rate in the state of Texas. Research shows that students who fail to complete high school are most likely to live in poverty as adults, are more likely to be convicted of criminal activity, and are more likely to suffer from substance abuse.

Good Use of Statistical Information to Emphasize Need

The Johnsonville School District has the highest high school dropout rate in the state of Texas. More than 18 percent of the district's students drop out of high school before completing 12th grade, compared to the state rate of 7 percent. Research shows that students who fail to complete high school are 50 percent more likely to live in poverty as adults than those who graduated from high school. They are 27 percent more likely to be convicted of criminal activity as adults than those who graduated from high school, and they are 22 percent more likely to suffer from substance abuse during their lifetime than those who graduated from high school.

The first example does an adequate job of identifying the need/stating the problem and citing research to demonstrate why the high dropout rate is a problem. But the second example does a better job by using statistics to emphasize the severity of the need and to answer the questions how severe, how many, and how much. In three sentences it has not only told funders that the dropout rate is high, but also told them how high by comparing it to another indicator (the state rate). It has also conveyed to the funder what is likely to happen as a result of dropping out of high school by providing statistics that demonstrate how many students who drop out are likely to suffer adverse consequences compared to those who complete high school.

Here are a few final tips to consider when creating your proposal's needs statement:

- As I suggested for the organizational description, maintain a file or several files of reports, statistical information, and needs assessments to use in your grant proposals. Remember to update the information regularly. If you continually compile this information, you will not have to spend countless hours looking for statistics when it is time to write a proposal.

- Cite your sources. This gives your proposal credibility and does not make the funder/proposal reviewer question where the numbers came from or doubt their accuracy.

- Often anecdotal information is effective and appropriate to use in a grant proposal, particularly if the funder is not a government agency. It is fine to use testimonials from clients to support your program, but, as with statistics, do not overuse them. Make sure that there is some quantitative data to provide balance and keep it relevant.

5. PROGRAM DESCRIPTION

The **program description** is second to the needs statement in importance. Once you've convinced the funder that a need truly exists, you must then devise a plan to address that need. If your plan to address the need and solve the problem appears unfeasible, weak, or poorly planned, it's unlikely that your proposal will be funded.

Let me elaborate. In my experience with grants, I have found that establishing the need is often the easy part. There are so many worthwhile causes and unaddressed problems that it is nearly always easy to identify a need. Sometimes it takes some work to convey that need to the funder, but that's where the art of writing the proposal comes in. However, I have also found that it is in the program description that many grant writers falter. A good, solid project design will win you the grant, but if you do not have a well-thought-out, fully developed program, you are significantly hurting your chances of securing grant funding.

The grant writer doesn't win you the grant; the project design wins you the grant. The grant proposal merely serves as a well-written articulation of the project.

There is a big difference between program development and proposal development. My focus is proposal development. This book will not tell you how to plan and design programs. I assume that your organization is able to design programs that address the needs of the population you are serving. If you need information on designing programs for social services, education, etc., you should consult any of the numerous books and instructional manuals on the subject.

The design of your program will influence the contents of the program description section of your grant proposal. You explained what the problem is in your needs statement. Now, in your program description, you must answer the following five questions:

- What are you going to do about it?

- Why are you doing it?

- How are you going to do it?

- Who is going to do it?

- When is it going to happen?

The level of detail in the program description will be dictated by the type of grant, as well as by any limitations placed on length by the funding guidelines or RFP. (Another way to gauge length is the point value assigned to the section. I'll speak to this in section **2.1a** of Chapter 6.)

Funders use various names to identify the information they wish applicants to include in their grant proposals. Here is a list of the common names for this information, linked to the five questions above so that you have a complete picture of all that you need to address in the program description:

- *Solution.* (What are you going to do about the problem identified in the needs section?)

- *Review of the literature/Best practices.* (Why did you decide on this solution?)

- *Goals/Objectives/Activities/Outcomes.* (How are you going to accomplish the project?)

- *Program/Project personnel.* (Who is going to administer the project?)

- *Timeline/Schedule of activities.* (When will the project take place?)

When writing your proposal, use the same topic headings the funder uses. Use the same language the funder uses to define your need and the subject matter of the project.

5.1 Solution

In the solution section, the grant writer needs to tell the funder what your organization will do to address the problem by laying out the design of the project. For example, you may start the program description with a paragraph like this:

The Johnsonville School District will address the problem of the district's double-digit dropout rate by implementing the Johnsonville's Kids Stay in School Program. The purpose of the Stay in School Program is to reduce the 18 percent dropout rate in the district by providing students at high risk of dropping out of high school with individual tutoring, mentoring, paid work experiences, and opportunities for participation in activities outside of school. It will also provide outreach to parents of high-risk students.

5.2 Review of the Literature/Best Practices

The literature review is a logical extension of the solution. This is where you explain why your organization decided on its chosen solution for addressing the problem. You will often find that your discussion of research and best practices picks up right where identifying the solution leaves off.

It should go without saying that your organization would not knowingly design, plan, or implement a program that had no chance of solving the problem it was created to address. In order to find out how other people in the field are dealing with the same problem, what's working, and what's not, read the literature (i.e., journals, magazines, books, newspapers, newsletters, websites). Best practices are simply the methods that have worked most successfully. You want to find out what they are and duplicate them (with modifications for your particular situation if necessary).

You should cite the results of your literature review and any best practices in your grant proposal because granting organizations are reluctant to fund programs that are not based upon reliable research in the field. They want to make sure they are funding a project that has a reasonable chance of solving whatever the problem may be. They want proof that the organization they are funding knows about the issue for which the funding is being sought. The literature review portion of your program description might look like this:

Research from the American Academy for the Promotion of High School Graduation shows that students who fail to complete high school drop out due to —

- failing grades,

- a lack of interest in school, and

- a lack of parental support.

The Johnsonville School District has conducted research on students who have dropped out of the district's high schools in the past three years and has found that more than 82 percent had failed at least three requisite courses their freshman year or were failing their third requisite course at the time that they stopped attending school. A South State

University study of high school dropouts suggests that once students are failing or have failed their third requisite course, there is a 60 percent greater chance that that student will drop out of high school versus a student who fails only one or two of these courses. Johnsonville's experiences appear to back up this claim.

As a result, the Stay in School Program will focus on freshman students who are failing or have failed one of the four requisite courses — Algebra I, English I, American History, or Biology. To address the issue of a lack of interest in high school, the Stay in School Program has based its project design on research in the field which suggests that students who are given paid internship opportunities, as well as the opportunity to participate in activities outside of school tied to grades, are three times more likely to graduate from high school. Additionally, educational institutions have always used outreach to parents, which stimulates parent/child interaction and engages parents and students in a dialogue about the value of staying in school, as a valuable tool to deter students from dropping out of school.

5.3 Goals/Objectives/Activities/ Outcomes

The section in which you discuss goals, objectives, activities, and outcomes is the meat of your program description. In this section you discuss, in detail, exactly how this project is going to work, step by step. Funders often refer to this section as "Methodology" or "Plan of Operation," but it is then further subdivided into the following categories:

- *Goals:* A goal is what your organization expects to accomplish with your program. Goals generally are broad statements. However, they should not be confused with the broad vision or mission of the organization. For our purposes, goals refer only to what you want to achieve with the program for which you are seeking grant funding.

- *Objectives:* A true objective is a measurement of what the organization will do to accomplish or move toward its stated goal. Objectives are quantifiable and measurable. They speak to the process used to achieve the goal. They often tell "how many" or "how much."

- *Activities:* Activities refer to specific tasks or strategies used to achieve each objective and are sometimes referred to as "process objectives."

- *Outcomes:* Outcomes differ from objectives in that they measure change as a result of a program's existence, thereby accomplishing or moving toward the stated goal. Outcomes are also quantifiable and measurable.

You will probably find that the terms "goals," "objectives," "outcomes," and "activities" are often misused or used interchangeably from one grant application to the next. Many funders don't distinguish between goals and objectives at all and consider them one and the same. Some funders do not distinguish between objectives and outcomes, while others see a distinct separation between the two. Keep that in mind as you approach each new grant application. The following example shows the terms used properly, as defined above.

Goal: The first goal of the Johnsonville Kids Stay in School Program is to decrease the dropout rate in the district.

Objective 1: Each of the district's high schools will hold 54 tutoring sessions (twice a week for 27 weeks) for at-risk students during the 2009–2010 school year.

Activity 1.1: Each high school will designate a tutor coordinator for the program.

Activity 1.2: The tutor coordinator for each high school will recruit 15 students to serve as tutors for each of the four requisite courses.

Activity 1.3: The tutor coordinator for each high school will identify all students who are earning a grade of D or F in any of the four requisite courses.

Activity 1.4: The tutor coordinator for each high school will establish a twice-weekly tutoring schedule for students identified in Activity 1.3 to receive tutoring in necessary course(s).

Objective 2: Each of the district's high schools will provide 100 of its at-risk students with mentors during the 2009–2010 school year.

Activity 2.1: Each high school will designate a mentor coordinator for the program.

Activity 2.2: The mentor coordinator for each high school will devise a system to select 100 at-risk students for the mentoring component of the program.

Activity 2.3: The mentor coordinator for each high school will recruit at least 50 adults from the community to serve as mentors to the selected at-risk students.

Activity 2.4: The mentor coordinator for each high school will pair each of the 100 students participating in the mentoring component of the program with an adult mentor.

Objective 3: Each of the district's high schools will provide 25 of its at-risk students with paid work experiences during the 2009–2010 school year.

Activity 3.1: Each high school will designate an internship coordinator for the program.

Activity 3.2: The internship coordinator for each high school will devise a system to select 25 at-risk students to participate in a paid work experience.

Activity 3.3: The internship coordinator for each high school will recruit 25 businesses and other organizations to serve as worksites for students participating in the internship component of the program.

Activity 3.4: The internship coordinator for each high school will place each of the 25 students participating in the internship component of the program with a business or other organization.

Worksheet 5 gives you a chance to come up with activities. Using the examples from Objectives 1 to 3, what do you think the activities to support Objectives 4 and 5 would look like?

Finally, let's discuss outcomes, which are arguably the most important of the four concepts. Why are outcomes so important? Well, in a word … success. Each outcome (as I've defined the term in this book) is an indicator that measures the success or failure of your program and is very important to the evaluation process, which we will discuss in section

6. You can use objectives to evaluate your program — they demonstrate the level of service that your organization performed for a particular program. However, it is the outcomes, sometimes referred to as "outcome objectives," that ultimately determine whether your program met its stated goal.

For example, look back at the examples for the goal and first objective. While it is important to know that because of the Stay in School Program, each of the Johnsonville School District's high schools held 54 tutoring sessions during the school year, what does that information really convey as it relates to achieving the goal of the program, decreasing the dropout rate? Not much. The following outcomes would provide a much better measure of success:

Outcome 1A: By the end of the first eight weeks of tutoring, 50 percent of students attending the twice-weekly tutoring sessions will improve their letter grade in each course for which they are being tutored.

Outcome 1B: At the end of 16 weeks of tutoring, 50 percent of students will be earning a C or better in each course for which they are being tutored.

This information is much more useful when evaluating the progress of the program toward meeting its stated goal. If 50 percent of students receiving tutoring raise their grades to a C level or better, then the program has lowered these students' risk of dropping out of high school. This is proof that the program is working and that progress is being made toward achieving the goal.

Here are two more examples of outcomes for the second and third objectives:

Outcome 2A: 75 percent of at-risk students assigned mentors during the school year will demonstrate improved attendance.

Outcome 2B: 80 percent of at-risk students assigned mentors during the school year will return to school the following school year.

Outcome 3A: 75 percent of at-risk students participating in paid work experiences during the school year will demonstrate improved attendance.

Outcome 3B: 85 percent of at-risk students participating in paid work experiences during the school year will return to school the following school year.

A final word on goals, objectives, activities, and outcomes: All concepts except for goals are written in future tense. You are almost always writing a proposal for a project that does not yet exist, so while the goal is stated in the present tense because it's what you want to do right now, everything else is stated in future tense because you are proposing what the program will do and projecting what the results will be (in the future) if you get the funding.

ESTABLISHING ACTIVITIES

Objective 4: Each of the district's high schools will organize a total of six free activities outside of school during the 2009–2010 school year (two for each nine-week period, beginning the second nine weeks of school).

Activity 4.1: _____

_____

Activity 4.2: _____

_____

Activity 4.3: _____

_____

Activity 4.4: _____

Objective 5: Each of the district's high schools will contact the parents of all its at-risk students during the 2009–2010 school year to share strategies for encouraging students to stay in school.

Activity 5.1: _____

_____

Activity 5.2: _____

_____

Activity 5.3: _____

_____

Activity 5.4: _____

_____

Grant proposals should be edited for consistency, clarity, and brevity.

5.4 Program/Project Personnel

The personnel section of the program description is one of the more painless sections to write. The funder wants the following information:

- Who is in charge of the project?

- Who else will be working on it?

- What qualifications must individuals working in this program possess?

- What are the qualifications of the staff identified to work on the project?

- Will project staff be drawn from personnel already working at your organization or must staff be hired after grant funds are awarded?

- Will the project staff be paid from grant funds, from other sources of funding, from a combination of funding sources, or will they serve as unpaid volunteers?

Some grant applications will request full job descriptions. Others will simply ask for an abbreviated version of major job duties. Many federal grant programs want a full résumé or vita for project staff, particularly the project director or principal investigator. Although most scientific, technical, and research grants are awarded to a particular institution, it is the specialized experience, knowledge, skills, and/or abilities of the Principal Investigator (PI) that are essential to writing and winning the grant award. You do not hire a PI for these grants after the grant is awarded. Without a solid, qualified PI with the necessary background, experience, and expertise already in place at the institution, no grant will be awarded.

Adhere to the RFP or application guidelines when writing and compiling this section of the program description. Your ultimate goal is to assure the funding agency that your organization currently has or will hire the proper staff to conduct the program, and that the staff will be credentialed, qualified, and in possession of the appropriate skills to handle the project and its target population.

In addition to identifying the key personnel, supplying evidence of their qualifications, and describing their job duties, you will often be asked to include a copy of the organizational chart. The funding agency wants to see how your organization is structured, where the grant project will be located on the "organizational food chain," and where (i.e., how high up) project personnel are located in the hierarchy. The funder is interested in the level of priority the grant project holds within the grant-seeking institution, and the organizational chart provides evidence of the applicant organization's commitment to the project.

5.5 Timeline/Schedule of Activities

The timeline, also called the schedule of activities, is as simple as it sounds. This section of the program description details what you are going to do and when you are going to do it. Providing a timeline of program activity conveys to the funder that you are organized and that you have planned out the life of the grant-funded program. You know what you are going to do and when you would like to, or need to, have each task accomplished to meet the program's goals. A timeline is required for most grant proposals, and grant reviewers will take it into account when deciding whether or not to award funding to your organization.

Of course, once grant funds have been awarded, every well-laid-out plan can change, and funders understand that organizations cannot always control the pace at which tasks are accomplished. However, failing to construct a timeline well before you undertake a major project will make it even more likely that you'll face delays, unexpected road-blocks, and full-out disasters because you've forgotten to allow for holidays or have underestimated how long something will take. Remember that grant funds are awarded for a limited time period, and if your organization is funded, it needs a plan to follow in order to stay on task. Timely completion of program activities and goals is necessary to fulfill your obligations to the funder and, if you have received a multiyear award, to receive funding for the following year.

Use your goals/objectives/activities/outcomes to create your timeline. I like to organize the information in a chart or table (see Sample 8). This helps you arrange the information more clearly and makes it easier for the grant reviewers to read and understand. List your goals/objectives/activities/outcomes (using the terminology of the funder), and beside each activity indicate either when it will take place (if it's ongoing) or when it will be completed.

 Break up lengthy proposal narratives with tables, charts, graphs, and maps. They are easier to read and also provide quick comparisons of data. Also use bulleted lists and bold headings.

Identify which staff will be responsible for completing each task. List them by job title rather than by name, just in case you hire a new person between the time you apply for a

grant and the time you receive funding. Providing this information requires that you think through how the program will work — not just the sometimes abstract design of the program, but the tangible details of how it will run. This will ensure that all program staff are clear about their roles and responsibilities.

Finally, list the program outcomes and a date by which you will achieve each outcome. The funder may not expect you to give a specific date of completion, but a range of dates, or a season or semester (for academic institutions), will work just fine (i.e., "by the end of the spring term" instead of "April 15, 20--").

6. EVALUATION PLAN

The **evaluation plan** is one of the most dreaded sections of a grant application. It is important because this is where the value of your proposed project will shine through ... or not. The evaluation plan is all about getting to the results and assessing your program's impacts. It is, of course, aligned with the goals/objectives/activities/outcomes section of the proposal and should be designed to show the funding agency how you will measure, analyze, and communicate the effectiveness of your project.

6.1 Internal versus External

Before we get to the specifics, you need to think about who will conduct the evaluation. A common question is, "Do I need an external evaluator to assess the effectiveness of my program?" As with everything else, it depends. Often the funder, particularly the federal government, will require that grantees have an external evaluator, but not always. This is generally a requirement when the program is

PROGRAM TIMELINE

Timeline for the Johnsonville Public School District's Kids Stay in School Program

Goal: The first goal of the Johnsonville Kids Stay in School Program is to decrease the dropout rate in the district.

Objective 1: Each of the district's high schools will hold 54 tutoring sessions (two per week for 27 weeks) for at-risk students during the 2009–2010 school year.

Activity/Outcome	Implementation Date	Parties Responsible
Activity 1.1: Each high school will designate a tutor coordinator for the program.	End of September 2009	High school principals
Activity 1.2: The tutor coordinator for each high school will recruit 15 students to serve as tutors for each of the four requisite courses.	Mid-October 2009	Tutor coordinator at each high school
Activity 1.3: The tutor coordinator for each high school will identify all students who are earning a grade of D or F in any of the four requisite courses.	End of first nine weeks of school year (end of October 2009)	Tutor coordinator at each high school
Activity 1.4: The tutor coordinator for each high school will establish a twice-weekly tutoring schedule for students identified in Activity 1.3 to receive tutoring in necessary course(s).	Start of second nine-week period of school year (November 1, 2009)	Tutor coordinator at each high school
Outcome 1A: By the end of the first eight weeks of tutoring, 50 percent of students attending the twice-weekly tutoring sessions will improve their letter grade in each course for which they are being tutored.	End of December 2009	Tutor coordinator at each high school to collect information; external evaluator to evaluate it
Outcome 1B: At the end of 16 weeks of tutoring, 50 percent of students will be earning a C or better in each course for which they are being tutored.	End of February 2010	Tutor coordinator at each high school to collect information; external evaluator to evaluate it

broad or far-reaching and complex, and/or when the financial award is large (hundreds of thousands of dollars or more). Some federal agencies just prefer that grantees use an external evaluator. Some foundations may also stipulate that grantees use an external evaluator, but I have found this to be less common.

To determine what your organization should do, first look at the RFP or application instructions. You may not be given a choice. However, if the application materials do not stipulate a preference, my first choice would be to have my program assessed externally. I equate an "external evaluation" with an "audit" or other investigation of a public or private sector organization. How good are we at policing ourselves? Is it in our best interests to do so? There is a reason why independent audits are conducted. It is more credible to have an independent, outside entity or individual carry out these types of activities. It is the same thing with using an external evaluator. Using an individual with no stake in the results of the evaluation gives the appearance of a transparent, objective, unbiased assessment of your program.

The federal government often allows organizations to budget grant funds for the costs of hiring an external evaluator. There are some grant programs, however, that do not. Foundations will vary.

If there are no available grant funds to cover the cost of an external evaluator, a second option, for smaller programs, would be to seek out an evaluator from the community who is willing to donate his or her time to conduct the program evaluation. Teachers and college and university professors are excellent candidates.

A third option would be to enlist colleagues in your field or peers at other organizations similar to yours to serve as evaluators. For example, the colleges in my area that have US Department of Education TRIO grants use directors from one another's programs as evaluators.

A fourth option is to simply evaluate your program internally, using an in-house evaluator or a group of staff members to monitor the program. Internal evaluation of grant programs is common and perfectly acceptable unless the funder has issues with it. It may be difficult for smaller organizations to track and compile the necessary information, depending on the scope of the project, but once a system is put in place, the evaluation becomes all about consistent collection of the necessary program data and giving staff time to assess the data.

At larger organizations, particularly colleges and universities, there is usually an office of research, planning, or institutional effectiveness, staffed by people with degrees in social science research, education, or statistics and/or with experience in program planning and evaluation or in organizational research and assessment. These offices exist to do research on, and collect data for, the institution's various programs and the populations that they serve. They use this data to evaluate the effectiveness of the organization and its programs. If you have access to one of these offices, it would be wise to ask the staff for help to design your evaluation plan and to serve as expert evaluators, internal to the organization, but external to the grant-funded project.

6.2 Quantitative versus Qualitative

When it comes to the actual mechanics of writing an evaluation plan, there are a couple of critical issues — whether the assessment is qualitative or quantitative (or both), and whether it is formative or summative (or both). We will first tackle the quantitative versus qualitative argument.

In a quantitative assessment, derived from the word "quantity," you evaluate your data using numbers. You use objective measures for data collection and report the impacts of the project numerically. In a qualitative assessment, derived from the word "quality," you will measure the program's quality, assessing the subjective impacts of the program on program participants or the target population.

Both quantitative and qualitative evaluations are important to the evaluation plan, and I try to employ both forms of assessment in the evaluation plans of any grant I write. They each provide program staff with valuable information about the functioning and effectiveness of the grant-funded program.

Your quantitative evaluation will reveal the bottom line. Did you meet your program goals or not? For example, if your organization received a grant to address the problem of juvenile crime in your area and one of your stated goals was to reduce the juvenile crime rate over a three-year period, 10 percent per year, your quantitative assessment would simply focus on whether you did or did not meet the goal of reducing the juvenile crime rate over three years and whether you did or did not meet your stated outcome of reducing the juvenile crime by 10 percent each year.

You would know what the juvenile crime rate was in your area before the program began, and you would have designed the program based on this information. Each year your program was in operation, you would obtain the latest statistics on juvenile crime rates. When it came time to evaluate the program, you would ask, "Did the rate decline? If so, by how much — 2 percent, 5 percent, 10 percent?" This is a quantitative measure of whether your program reached its goal ... a clear indication of whether or not your program is working.

It may be that your program is making progress toward achieving the overall (and more general) goal of reducing the juvenile crime rate in the area, but is falling short of meeting the outcomes as stated in the grant proposal. For example, you may see a decline in the juvenile crime rate of 5 percent instead of 10 percent. It is still a decline, but not to the extent you projected. This information is useful and should be included in the evaluation reports and communicated to the funder.

This is how best practices are created and communicated to others in your field. Obtaining this information will also allow you to give extra support to those aspects of your program that are working, and to further analyze and correct those that aren't working. Did you set the expectations for your outcomes too high? Are there other factors contributing to the lower results than you expected? What can you change to produce better results?

A qualitative evaluation of the same program would focus on the perceptions and experiences of program participants. It would rely heavily on interviews and surveys for data. This is subjective, but written and spoken feedback, as well as observable behavior, are good indicators of the effects a program is having on its participants. For example, if a teenager, prior to entering the program, was constantly in trouble at school, failed to complete schoolwork, or was picked up for truancy or curfew violations, and if he or she demonstrated a positive change in attitude and/or behavior after participating in the program, this would demonstrate a positive outcome of the program. If the teenager indicated in a survey or interview that he or she now attends classes regularly, rarely gets into trouble, and likes coming to the program and participating in its activities, the evaluation report would detail the qualitative success of the program.

Qualitative evaluations also give you an opportunity to make necessary adjustments to improve program procedures and activities. Some qualitative feedback may be negative, providing you with valuable information about flaws in the way the program is run. You can use this information to make continual improvements to advance the goal of the program.

6.3 Formative versus Summative

Just as using both the quantitative and qualitative methods of evaluation has its benefits, so too does using both formative and summative evaluation processes.

A formative evaluation is a continual, ongoing process that assesses the effectiveness of project activities. It measures how successfully the program is making progress toward achieving its objectives. A formative evaluation requires that program staff devise a regular schedule to collect and document data pertaining to whether activities are being conducted and how well they are achieving the desired outcomes.

A summative evaluation, on the other hand, refers to the final results achieved by your program as opposed to the process. What is meant by "final results" will vary depending on how the goals/objectives/activities/outcomes section is written. For example, if you have a three-year grant, your summative evaluation will evaluate the results of the program at the end of the three-year period, but you have likely designed the program to achieve specific outcomes at various stages along the three-year timeline. Your summative evaluation will measure these outcomes as well. Look again at the timeline in Sample 8.

In a formative evaluation, you will assess the activities. For example:

- Are Activities 1.1 to 1.4 being conducted?

- Are Activities 1.1 to 1.4 being conducted according to the specified implementation date in the timeline?

- Have all of the four activities been completed or are they partially completed or incomplete leading up to the implementation date? Why?

- Have you collected the appropriate data on the steps being taken to complete Activities 1.1 to 1.4 and has this been documented?

For a summative evaluation, you will look at the outcomes. For example:

- Have Outcomes 1A and 1B been achieved?

- Were Outcomes 1A and 1B achieved according to the specified implementation dates in the timeline? Why or why not?

- What are the results of each outcome, quantitatively? Were the projected outcomes realistic or should they be adjusted?

- Was the appropriate data collected to verify and document the outcomes?

6.4 Data Collection/Evaluation Tools

The final part of the evaluation plan is the actual collection of the data, commonly referred to as the evaluation tools. You need to detail what data will be collected to conduct the evaluation and how you will collect it. For example:

Activity 1.2: The tutor coordinator for each high school will recruit 15 students to serve as tutors for each of the four requisite courses.

To measure the progress toward completing this activity, the tutor coordinator might create an application form that students wishing to become tutors can complete. The application process may consist of the application form, a grade check, and an interview. At the end of the selection process, the tutor coordinator would collect the students' application forms, copies of their most recent report cards, and page of notes or a checklist from each interview conducted and would place them in a file with the list of those selected to be student tutors. This is an example of data collection and documentation. These items are your evaluation tools.

Outcome 1B: At the end of 16 weeks of tutoring, 50 percent of students will be earning a C or better in each course for which they are being tutored.

In this example, the tutor coordinator would obtain from the school or from individual teachers a current report card or progress report on each student in each course for which they are receiving tutoring assistance. It was established in Activity 1.3 that those students selected for tutoring were earning a grade of D or F in at least one of the four requisite courses. The tutor coordinator would obtain a record of those grades, and at the intervals established in the grant, he or she would obtain and evaluate records of student grades to measure each student's progress toward achieving the outcome. This would allow him or her to determine whether or not the program had been effective in reaching the quantitative measurement established in the grant. This information should be documented and a record maintained.

6.5 Some Final Tips

Writing the evaluation plan of a grant proposal seems difficult at first glance, but "cumbersome" is probably a more accurate word to describe the process. How cumbersome it is will depend on the length of the proposal and the complexity of the grant program. Some grant programs have several goals and objectives and activities and outcomes. Others do not have nearly as many.

I have tried to present this process in a logical, step-by-step manner — methodically — which is how I suggest you design and write your entire grant proposal. If you use this approach, you will notice that each section of the grant informs the other sections, and they flow logically from one to the other. Though I did state at the beginning of this chapter that you do not have to write the various sections of a grant proposal in order, it goes without saying that you should write the program description before you focus on the evaluation plan. You need to know how the program is put together before you can evaluate it. As I've said before, grant writing is a process.

 Make sure that your proposal uses the same terms consistently throughout and that each section informs all others.

You might find it easier to organize your evaluation plan if you put the information into a chart or table. And keep the following points in mind:

- Use your program's goals/objectives/activities/outcomes as the basis for your evaluation.

- Determine what type of evaluation tools you will use — in other words, know what data you will need to collect.

- Know how often the data will need to be collected.

- Determine who will collect the information and how it will be maintained or stored.

- Use a combination quantitative and qualitative evaluation.

- Use both formative and summative evaluation methods.

- Determine whether or not you will use an internal or external evaluator.

 Grant proposals should be neat, free of typos, and well presented. Even though you use "spell check" and "grammar check," you still need to proofread.

7. OTHER COMMON GRANT PROPOSAL SECTIONS

There are other sections that are often included in grant proposals but that vary from funding source to funding source. Sometimes you may be required to include them per the RFP or application instructions, other times you will not.

7.1 Cover Letter/Cover Page/ Table of Contents

Some funders require applicant organizations to attach a **cover letter** to be submitted with their grant proposals. The cover letter goes on top and will be the first thing the funder and/or proposal reviewer sees. It does not need to contain any earth-shattering information (see Sample 9).

Use your organization's letterhead. Introduce your organization as the applicant for "XYZ Federal Grant Program." State that you are seeking funding for [*insert program name*] to support "ABC" activities. Briefly state the major goals of your program. Identify any relevant partnerships or collaborations. Mention the organization's contribution(s) to the program and thank the funder for reviewing your application. The letter should be signed by an authorized official (the president, CEO, or executive director of the organization).

The **cover page** of a grant proposal will vary depending on the grant program. Some funders will create a cover page form for applicants to fill out and place at the beginning of the proposal. Other funders will simply

Carter University
1273 College Avenue
Oklahoma City, OK 73261

July 1, 2009

Ms. Elizabeth Smith, Program Officer
United States Department of Education
789 Lincoln Square
Washington, DC 77777

Dear Ms. Smith:

Please find enclosed Carter University's grant application for your agency's Teacher Preparation and Development grant program. The university's College of Education is seeking funding to support its new initiative, Science Teachers' Opportunities Program or STOP. The STOP Initiative has three main goals:

- To recruit more students into the science education program at Carter University

- To provide additional training in science curriculum to practicing science teachers

- To improve the standardized test scores of secondary students in science in the state of Oklahoma

Carter University will be partnering with the local community college district, consisting of three colleges in the surrounding area — Danielle Community College, Eric Community College, and Chanel Community College. We will be working with the community colleges to identify students interested in teaching who are planning on transferring to a four-year university to obtain a bachelor's degree in an effort to recruit these students to Carter's science education program.

In addition, the STOP Initiative will collaborate with science teachers from the three largest school districts in the area, with plans to expand statewide. We will concentrate our efforts on middle school science teachers and offer in-service and summer workshops focusing on enhancing the science curriculum at that level with an emphasis on hands-on teaching, anticipating that improvements in this area will increase students' standardized test scores.

Carter University will contribute the time of ten full-time faculty from its College of Education, as well as the time of six graduate assistants, to the project. The university is also supporting the program through dedicated office space and equipment and access to university vehicles for travel to support program activities.

Thank you for your consideration of our proposal.

Sincerely,

Johnnie Jones

Dr. Johnnie Jones, President

inform applicants in the instructions that they should include a cover page with their proposals and will tell them what information it should contain. The federal government has a standard form, SF-424, which is used by numerous grant programs across several federal agencies as a universally accepted cover page (see Sample 10).

Some funders, especially federal agencies, will require applicants to create a **table of contents** for their grant proposals. The lengthier the proposal, the more useful a table of contents is to the reviewers. Some funders will give applicants a specified format or even provide a form for them to use. Some electronic proposal submission systems (see section **1.3** of Chapter 6) will create the table of contents for you, based on the information entered elsewhere in the proposal.

Follow the funder's guidelines when creating your table of contents. Every page of the grant proposal should be numbered consecutively. Place all sections of the grant in order according to funder guidelines and use this order to create the table of contents. Every item in the grant should be placed in the table of contents with a corresponding page number or page range. Place the table of contents at the front of the grant proposal, after the cover letter, cover page, and abstract. (Because these sections come before the table of contents, they do not have to be included on the contents page, though I myself like to include everything.)

7.2 Letters of Support/Attachments/ Appendixes

Not all funders request that applicants submit **letters of support**, but a very large number do, and if they are written correctly, letters of support will lend credibility to your grant applications (see Sample 11). They can come from a variety of sources, including, but not limited to, partners, project collaborators, community-based organizations, elected officials, religious organizations, other departments within your organization (if it is large enough to have several departments), and other organizations representing the target population.

Letters of support are not simple, benign statements such as: "Oh, I really like Bob. He's a great social worker, and if you give him the grant, I know he'll do a good job." Nor are they platitudes like: "We here at Community Based Organization admire the work being done by Grant Applicant and support the project as worthy and valuable to the community." Letters of support have to say something beyond "We support them." Do not request letters of support from irrelevant organizations that have no knowledge of your program's activities nor have any relation to the target population you serve. More is *not* more unless your letters have some substance. And you will not get extra points for having your state's senator or congressperson write a letter of support. Every organization does this. It does not have the effect you may think.

Your letters of support should be relevant and from key stakeholders, such as partners and representatives of, and advocates for, the target population. Letters of support should go beyond merely supporting a project. They should state a commitment to assist the applicant organization in meaningful ways as it implements the project, to help carry out project activities, or to provide resources to the target population. They are not just letters of support, but letters of commitment (which is another term sometimes used to describe them).

COVER PAGE — FEDERAL GOVERNMENT FORM SF-424

Application for Federal Assistance SF-424   Version 02

* 1. Type of Submission:

☐ Preapplication

☐ Application

☐ Changed/Corrected Application

* 2. Type of Application:

☐ New

☐ Continuation

☐ Revision

* If Revision, select appropriate letter(s):

* Other (Specify)

* 3. Date Received:

| Completed by Grants.gov upon submission. |

4. Applicant Identifier:

5a. Federal Entity Identifier:

* 5b. Federal Award Identifier:

State Use Only:

6. Date Received by State:

7. State Application Identifier:

8. APPLICANT INFORMATION:

* a. Legal Name:

* b. Employer/Taxpayer Identification Number (EIN/TIN):

* c. Organizational DUNS:

d. Address:

* Street1:

Street2:

* City:

County:

* State:

Province:

* Country: USA: UNITED STATES

* Zip / Postal Code:

e. Organizational Unit:

Department Name:

Division Name:

f. Name and contact information of person to be contacted on matters involving this application:

Prefix: *** First Name:**

Middle Name:

* Last Name:

Suffix:

Title:

Organizational Affiliation:

* Telephone Number: Fax Number:

* Email:

Application for Federal Assistance SF-424 Version 02

9. Type of Applicant 1: Select Applicant Type:

Type of Applicant 2: Select Applicant Type:

Type of Applicant 3: Select Applicant Type:

* Other (specify):

* **10. Name of Federal Agency:**

NGMS Agency

11. Catalog of Federal Domestic Assistance Number:

CFDA Title:

* **12. Funding Opportunity Number:**

MBL-SF424FAMILY-ALLFORMS

* Title:

MBL-SF424Family-AllForms

13. Competition Identification Number:

Title:

14. Areas Affected by Project (Cities, Counties, States, etc.):

* **15. Descriptive Title of Applicant's Project:**

Attach supporting documents as specified in agency instructions.

Application for Federal Assistance SF-424   Version 02

16. Congressional Districts Of:

* a. Applicant [   ]   * b. Program/Project [   ]

Attach an additional list of Program/Project Congressional Districts if needed.

[   ] [Add Attachment] [Delete Attachment] [View Attachment]

17. Proposed Project:

* a. Start Date: [   ]   * b. End Date: [   ]

18. Estimated Funding ($):

* a. Federal [   ]

* b. Applicant [   ]

* c. State [   ]

* d. Local [   ]

* e. Other [   ]

* f. Program Income [   ]

* g. TOTAL [   ]

* 19. Is Application Subject to Review By State Under Executive Order 12372 Process?

☐ a. This application was made available to the State under the Executive Order 12372 Process for review on [   ]

☐ b. Program is subject to E.O. 12372 but has not been selected by the State for review.

☐ c. Program is not covered by E.O. 12372.

* 20. Is the Applicant Delinquent On Any Federal Debt? (If "Yes", provide explanation.)

☐ Yes   ☐ No   [Explanation]

21. *By signing this application, I certify (1) to the statements contained in the list of certifications** and (2) that the statements herein are true, complete and accurate to the best of my knowledge. I also provide the required assurances** and agree to comply with any resulting terms if I accept an award. I am aware that any false, fictitious, or fraudulent statements or claims may subject me to criminal, civil, or administrative penalties. (U.S. Code, Title 218, Section 1001)

☐ **** I AGREE**

** The list of certifications and assurances, or an internet site where you may obtain this list, is contained in the announcement or agency specific instructions.

Authorized Representative:

Prefix: [   ]   * First Name: [   ]

Middle Name: [   ]

* Last Name: [   ]

Suffix: [   ]

* Title: [   ]

* Telephone Number: [   ]   Fax Number: [   ]

* Email: [   ]

* Signature of Authorized Representative: [Completed by Grants.gov upon submission.]   * Date Signed: [Completed by Grants.gov upon submission.]

Application for Federal Assistance SF-424

* Applicant Federal Debt Delinquency Explanation

The following field should contain an explanation if the Applicant organization is delinquent on any Federal Debt. Maximum number of characters that can be entered is 4,000. Try and avoid extra spaces and carriage returns to maximize the availability of space.

Big City Chamber of Commerce
110 Downtown Street
Big City, OK 54321

March 1, 2009

Mr. Jim Bean, Director of Labor Preparation
United States Department of Labor
123 Washington Boulevard
Washington, DC 77777

Dear Mr. Bean:

This letter is to support the "Big City Medical Manufacturing Workforce Initiative" grant proposal submitted by the Big City Career Technology Center. The Big City Career Technology Center plays a major role in the technical and career training and continuing education of Big City residents, providing training to 20 percent of the city's workforce at some time throughout their careers.

According to our annual "Big City Chamber Workforce Assessment," with the changing demographics of Big City and the growth of medical manufacturing companies in the area over the past five years, the availability of workers with the necessary training in technology-oriented medical manufacturing processes is limited. Big City is expected to experience a shortage of qualified workers to fill positions in these companies over the next five years.

If the growth of the industry continues at its current pace, Big City will require a 7 percent increase in trained workers over the next five years. The Big City Chamber of Commerce applauds the efforts of the Big City Career Technology Center in taking the lead in training workers for the medical manufacturing industry. By working with employers to design and implement targeted training programs to increase the number of workers in the industry, the Technology Center has positioned itself to meet the growing need in our city over the coming years.

The Big City Chamber of Commerce will support the activities of the "Big City Medical Manufacturing Workforce Initiative" with the following contributions:

- Providing a cash match not to exceed $50,000 to fund training stipends and tuition assistance for unemployed and underemployed workers.

- Assisting with the recruitment of unemployed and underemployed workers into the Medical Manufacturing Training Program.

- Networking with business and industry to form focus groups on industry needs and process improvements.

- Organizing the "Big City Metropolitan Area Medical Manufacturing Association," in an effort to promote economic development in the region.

Should this project meet the expectations of industry in the area, we look forward to continuing this collaboration beyond the funding period of the grant.

Thank you for your consideration.

Sincerely,

Bobby Jones

Mr. Bobby Jones, Executive Director
(987) 654-3210

Letters of support should be signed by a high-ranking official in the organization. This demonstrates commitment to the project from the top levels of an organization's hierarchy. However, strongly worded letters of support from those on the front lines, who have extensive experience working on the problem or with the target population, are equally effective.

Sometimes letters of support are considered part of the **attachments** section. Funding agencies use the words "Attachments" and "Appendixes" interchangeably to describe the supporting documentation an applicant may include to enhance a proposal. Some funders will demand that you include certain documents in addition to the narrative section of your grant proposal; others will accept attachments, but will not make them mandatory. They may limit the number of additional pages you can add. Still other funders will request that no attachments be sent at all. The application instructions will inform you of the wishes of your particular funder.

When the funder leaves it to the applicants' discretion, my advice is to be judicious in your selection and keep it relevant. The following list includes what may be considered attachments or appendixes to your grant proposal.

- IRS 501(c)(3) Determination Letter proving tax-exempt status

- Current annual operating budget

- Most recent financial statement (audited or unaudited)

- Most recent IRS Form 990

- Résumés and/or job descriptions of project personnel

- Organizational chart

- Maps of the organization's facilities

- List of the members of the governing board

- Examples of evaluation tools

- Copies of previous project reports

Pull together all attachments and appendixes well in advance. Be judicious when you choose the information that you will include. Make sure that it is relevant.

7.3 Management Plan/Plan of Operation

The **management plan** is another section common to grant proposals of all types. It may be a section all by itself or it could be combined with the goals/objectives/activities/outcomes and/or project personnel sections of the grant proposal. The management plan describes how the organization is structured, what resources are available within the organization to support the program, and how the program will be managed (there is an example of a management plan in the grant proposal of Appendix 1).

When writing the management plan, you will need to discuss what your organization looks like structurally. This is another opportunity to include the organizational chart if you have not done so previously. Point out who will supervise the program director and why this is the best and most logical place in the organizational structure to put the program. Talk about the various departments and other personnel within the organization that possess special resources that would benefit the program.

Most important, discuss the organization's ability to operate the project. If you are proposing a million-dollar project over a five-year period, you had better demonstrate that your organization has the capacity to handle a million-dollar project. Describe your human resources system, your finance system, and any specialized institution-wide software that makes managing such a large project easier. Demonstrate that you can handle the requirements for program evaluation and reporting. If your organization has previously managed large-scale projects like the one you are proposing, say so.

This section of the grant proposal should convince the funder that your organization —

- is dedicated to the success of the project (indicated by the project's placement within the organization and the resources dedicated to support it), and

- possesses the capacity to manage all the program and financial aspects of the project.

A management plan is sometimes referred to as a **plan of operation**. At other times the plan of operation will include certain aspects of the management plan as I defined it above, but with other funder-defined information as well. And then there are times when a funder requests a plan of operation when what it really wants are the portions of the proposal that I included in the program description section. The bottom line, as I've said several times throughout this chapter, is that every grant proposal is different, with different application instructions, program guidelines, formats, forms, and other requirements. This is why it is important for you to obtain funding guidelines, read and reread them, and comply with all application instructions and their respective requirements to the letter.

7.4 Dissemination Plan

Grant programs that are aimed at academic institutions commonly request a **dissemination plan**. However, many foundations naturally focus on new and better ways of doing things, so they too are interested in dissemination of results. These grant makers encourage innovation in program design and are always looking for a fresh approach to solving an old problem, especially if the problem has existed for a long time or is pervasive within a city, region, or state. For those funders, disseminating best practices is as important as the plan your organization has come up with to address the need itself.

Dissemination refers to how you get information out to others who are addressing the same or a similar problem. The purpose of dissemination is replication. You want as many other organizations as possible to know what you are doing in your program and what is having a positive effect on the need and the target population. (You may also want them to know what isn't working, so they can avoid these pitfalls.)

Of course, duplicating a project that is taking place in one area doesn't guarantee its success in another area. However, disseminating your results does provide a body of knowledge upon which to base other projects. Sometimes, instead of reproducing a project in its entirety, organizations will borrow elements of a project that have shown positive results. This is the importance of dissemination.

Your dissemination plan should indicate who will receive information on the successes and failures of your program, how this information will be distributed, and how expansive the network will be. I've suggested some answers to these questions:

- To whom will the results of the program be disseminated?
  - Funders
  - Peers/Colleagues in your field
  - Academia/Researchers
  - Policy makers/Government officials
- How will program results be disseminated?
  - Create a website
  - Publish and distribute a newsletter
  - Make presentations on program results at conferences and workshops
  - Create and distribute a video
  - Publish a book or manual on the subject

- Disburse materials and other tools used in the program
- How expansive will dissemination efforts be?
  - Local
  - Statewide
  - National

7.5 Certifications/Assurances/ Nondiscrimination Policies/ Equitable Access/Statement of Diversity/Other Forms

Federal grant programs require applicants to include a multitude of forms, written in legalese, that address a variety of issues for applicants to attest to. **Certifications** lay out requirements regarding lobbying, debarment and suspension, and drug-free workplace laws. There is often a separate required form called "Disclosure of Lobbying Activities" that is designed to — what else? — disclose the applicant organization's lobbying activities.

Assurances list a range of activities and compliance standards that applicant organizations must adhere to, from their eligibility to apply for federal funding to their compliance with federal environmental standards.

Some grant programs will request that applicants submit a copy of their organization's **nondiscrimination policy**. Make several copies of your organization's policy (they should be included in your employee manual or available from your human resources office) and put them in a file, or recreate the policy electronically and store it on your computer. You will need it again and again to submit with other federal grant applications. Do the same thing with your organization's **equitable access and participation policy**, which states how your organization ensures equal access to, and participation in, its programs and services for program beneficiaries affected by the six barriers identified by US statutes: gender, race, national origin, color, disability, and age. Grant programs designed to assist diverse populations often request your **statement of diversity**. This requires organizations to seek out qualified personnel who are from diverse backgrounds themselves and/or who have experience working with diverse populations. Depending on the grant program, **other forms** may cover subject matter specific to the grant program such as human subjects, vertebrate animals, etc.

 Keep a hard-copy file and an electronic file of all the "canned" information that you will need for most of your grant proposals. It should include these items:

- Organizational description
- IRS 501(c)(3) determination letter
- Current annual operating budget
- Past operating budgets
- Most recent financial statement
- Most recent IRS Form 990
- Résumés and/or job descriptions
- Organizational chart
- Maps of the organization's facilities
- List of the members of the governing board
- Examples of evaluation tools
- Copies of previous project reports

- Copies of the organization's nondiscrimination and equitable access and participation policies
- Common grant application forms

7.6 Authorizing Statutes/Code of Federal Regulations (CFR)/ Invitational Priority

The **authorizing statutes** are the federal laws from which federal grant programs are created. The statutes speak generally to a program's origin and intent. Before applying for a grant award, make sure that your organization meets and is comfortable with the requirements set forth in the program's authorizing statutes.

The **Code of Federal Regulations (CFR)** is a compilation of the rules and regulations governing every possible activity conducted by federal agencies. The CFR is divided into 50 titles spread among four volumes, each of which is updated annually. The complete contents of the CFR are located online at www.gpoaccess.gov/cfr.

The program-specific rules from the CFR are inserted in many federal grant application packets to provide the applicant with information on the grant program to which they are applying. The CFR citation is given, and often the entire section of the CFR for a particular grant program is included for use by the applicant. Having a program's rules right in front of you saves you from having to take the time to access the website and conduct a search to find answers to questions concerning the operations of a program. Some of the information in the CFR on grant programs includes general definitions and eligibility requirements, allowable costs and activities, information on what to include in proposals, etc. All federal grant programs will have their program rules codified in the CFR. It is a great resource for grant seekers.

The US Department of Education often uses an **invitational priority** in its numerous grant programs. This means it gives organizations extra points, as it reviews their proposals, for meeting a specific "invitational priority." In other words, the agency will establish a criteria or goal for addressing a specified need (such as giving special attention to the needs of traditionally underrepresented populations of students), and organizations submitting applications are required to address how the program that they are proposing will fulfill that need.

Sometimes federal grants will ask applicants to meet a competitive priority, which simply means that novice applicants (those who have never received a federal award under the program) are given preference in the review process. In other grant programs, an applicant's prior experience serving the target population will enhance its chances during the review phase.

5
JUSTIFY THOSE FUNDS!
THE GRANT PROPOSAL BUDGET

Now to one of the most dreaded parts of the grant application process — creating the budget. I find that applicants often make putting together a grant budget harder than it has to be. These are my three basic rules for writing grant proposal budgets:

- Itemize

- Obtain the actual costs

- Justify your numbers

Simple!

1. GRANT BUDGET

How much money should you ask for? If only it depended on the answer to the question "How much money do you need?" It seems that we always need more money than we can reasonably ask for, or more than the funder is willing to give us. So, let's start there.

In Chapter 2 we learned that, by referring to the *Federal Register* and RFPs from government agencies, grant seekers can find out either the range of federal grant awards to be given, the maximum dollar amount of each

grant to be funded, or both. I cannot remember a situation in my career where I have applied for a federal grant without knowing what the limits on funding were.

There are state and local government grants, however, that give grant seekers little or no indication of what to ask for. It is not unreasonable to contact the funder to ask. At other times, you may need to do a little sleuthing to reach a conclusion. For instance, a state grant program that my college applied for did not establish a funding cap on individual grant awards, but it did acknowledge that it was taking applications from nonprofit organizations all over the state. The maximum amount of funding in that program that fiscal year was $350,000, and the agency expected to make four to six grant awards. It didn't take a rocket scientist to figure out that grant budgets should be in the $58,000 to $87,000 range. I assumed that applicants who significantly exceeded $87,000 would not be funded. As it turned out, six grants were awarded and the largest grant was $75,000.

Foundations and corporate grant programs will generally give applicants a maximum dollar amount for grant requests, but some may not. In Chapter 2 I discussed using the foundation's annual reports and IRS Form 990 to determine which organizations the foundation contributed to in the past, for what types of projects, and how much it gave. Use this information to form your grant requests.

1.1 Itemize

When you begin creating your budget, use your program description as a guide (see section **5** of Chapter 4). Brainstorm. Think about the various elements of your program and what you will require to run it in terms of staff and supplies. What are your goals and objectives? What are your program activities? What outcomes do you plan on achieving? How do you get there and what resources will you need to accomplish all program tasks? Begin making a list of these items. Write down everything that you could possibly need money for and that would support the goals and objectives of your program. Sample 12 shows what a rough draft might look like.

Once you have the first list compiled, you will notice that some categories are broad and require further explanation. Go over the list a second time and break down costs that are lumped together. Go over the list a third time and compare it with your program description to make sure you haven't left out any activities.

The federal government lists the most common categories on its Standard Form 424A, which is a "universal" budget form used by some (but not all) federal agencies and grant programs. See Sample 13.

1.2 Obtain Actual Costs

As much as possible, grant seekers need to obtain the actual costs of projected program expenditures. The federal standard for establishing budgetary costs is that they be "necessary and reasonable," which seems vague or arbitrary to many grant seekers. However, if you can justify how you determined the cost of a particular item (translation: if you can show that the item and the cost you've assigned to it are necessary and reasonable), then you should not worry about meeting the standard.

The most important thing is that you be conservative, but do not shortchange yourself.

When creating your grant budget, keep in mind the federal standard of "necessary and reasonable." Itemize all expenses and do the extra work it takes to find actual costs. Never be tempted to make up numbers. You do not want to jeopardize your chance of receiving a grant award by asking for too much money or for expense items that are counter to the standard of necessary and reasonable; nor do you want to risk the success of a funded project by asking for too little money. Document everything and keep this documentation in a file so that if you ever need to go back and verify the source of a cost listed in your proposal, you can. It won't appear to the funder as if the numbers were pulled out of thin air. Finally, always justify your costs; I will show you how to do this in section **3**.

 Create a realistic budget. Do not ask for more money than you need.

SAMPLE 12
PRELIMINARY LIST OF BUDGET ITEMS

Johnsonville Kids Stay in School Program

Items to budget for include:

- Project director
- Nine coordinators — three per high school (three tutor coordinators, three mentor coordinators, three internship coordinators)
- Travel to 18 events per school year — 6 per high school
- Local travel for project personnel
- Parent outreach activities — College night/Awards banquet
- Printing costs — Applications, mailings, manuals
- Postage costs — Mailings to students, parents, mentors, internship sites
- Costs for telephone service/fax machine/Internet connection
- Outside evaluator
- Equipment (computers, copy machines)
- Supplies (office, tutoring)

I have included the most common budget cost categories below, and I provide some advice for determining costs in each category. Keep in mind that for multiyear grants, you should develop a separate budget for each year.

1.2a Personnel — salaries/fringe benefits

When it comes to personnel, determine if the positions will be partially or fully funded by the grant. What is the prevailing wage for the equivalent position at your organization or within the field in your region? Use the same method to calculate the salary of a grant-funded employee that you would use to establish the salary of any other employee new to the organization.

Sample 14 shows an example of salaries only, but you must not forget to include the fringe benefits for grant-funded employees. If you fail to budget for fringe benefits, you risk requesting too little money to support the personnel costs of your grant. Also, for each additional year of the grant budget, adjust the salaries for pay increases and for any potential increases in fringe benefits.

1.2b Travel

Include whatever travel is required to implement the activities of your project. It could be local, statewide, or national and should include expenses for mileage, airfare, per diem, and hotel accommodations. Estimate the number of miles that may be traveled to fulfill program activities, and use the current mileage calculation provided by your organization. Many state and local governmental entities are required to use the mileage and per diem rates established by their states. This rate changes annually, sometimes more often, but it will likely correspond to the mileage rate set by the federal Internal Revenue Service. Check the IRS website at www.irs.gov.

FEDERAL BUDGET FORM (SF-424A)

BUDGET INFORMATION - Non-Construction Programs

SECTION A - BUDGET SUMMARY

Grant Program Function or Activity (a)	Catalog of Federal Domestic Assistance Number (b)	Estimated Unobligated Funds		New or Revised Budget		
		Federal (c)	Non-Federal (d)	Federal (e)	Non-Federal (f)	Total (g)
1.		$	$	$	$	$
2.						
3.						
4.						
5. Totals		$	$	$	$	$

SECTION B - BUDGET CATEGORIES

6. Object Class Categories	GRANT PROGRAM, FUNCTION OR ACTIVITY				Total (5)
	(1)	(2)	(3)	(4)	
a. Personnel	$	$	$	$	$
b. Fringe Benefits					
c. Travel					
d. Equipment					
e. Supplies					
f. Contractual					
g. Construction					
h. Other					
i. Total Direct Charges (sum of 6a-6h)					
j. Indirect Charges					
k. TOTALS (sum of 6i and 6j)	$	$	$	$	$
7. Program Income	$	$	$	$	$

Authorized for Local Reproduction

Standard Form 424A (Rev. 7- 97)
Prescribed by OMB (Circular A.-102)

SECTION C - NON-FEDERAL RESOURCES

(a) Grant Program	(b) Applicant	(c) State	(d) Other Sources	(e) TOTALS
8.	$	$	$	$
9.				
10.				
11.				
12. TOTAL (sum of lines 8-11)	$	$	$	$

SECTION D - FORECASTED CASH NEEDS

	Total for 1st Year	1st Quarter	2nd Quarter	3rd Quarter	4th Quarter
13. Federal	$	$	$	$	$
14. Non-Federal	$				
15. TOTAL (sum of lines 13 and 14)	$	$	$	$	$

SECTION E - BUDGET ESTIMATES OF FEDERAL FUNDS NEEDED FOR BALANCE OF THE PROJECT

(a) Grant Program	FUTURE FUNDING PERIODS (Years)			
	(b) First	(c) Second	(d) Third	(e) Fourth
16.	$	$	$	$
17.				
18.				
19.				
20. TOTAL (sum of lines 16 - 19)	$	$	$	$

SECTION F - OTHER BUDGET INFORMATION

21. Direct Charges:	22. Indirect Charges:
23. Remarks:	

Authorized for Local Reproduction

Standard Form 424A (Rev. 7-97) Page 2

PERSONNEL COSTS FOR PROPOSAL BUDGET

Year 1 Salaries			
1 Project Director	Full time @ $50,000 per year	100% grant funded	$50,000
3 Tutor Coordinators	Full time @ $30,000 per year	100% grant funded	$90,000
3 Mentor Coordinators	Full time @ $26,500 per year	100% grant funded	$79,500
3 Internship Coordinators	Part time @ $13,500 per year	100% grant funded	$40,500
3 Clerical Assistants	Full time @ $20,500 per year	50% grant funded	$30,750
Total Year 1 Salaries			**$290,750**

For airfare and hotel accommodations, use information supplied by your organization's purchasing officer or designated travel agency. Simply request a direct quote. For instance, "How much would it cost for two people to travel to a conference in Washington, DC, for two days?" These quotes will be reliable enough to use in your proposal budget.

1.2c Communications

Communications includes the cost of telephone service, including long distance and a fax line, postage, couriers, Internet connections, etc. Remember to use actual costs for all items where possible, and estimate where necessary. For example: Postage = 1,000 promotional fliers x $0.37 per flier = $370. Remember to watch for US Postal Service rate increases, and for multi-year budgets calculate postage costs at the anticipated higher rate. Similar to mileage, postage rate increases are becoming a common occurrence and can be quite costly.

Also, remember that all communications costs should directly support the activities of the grant-funded program and are not to be used to support the general expenses of the organization. If a grant-funded program is using your organization's existing phone line, for example, you must estimate how much time the program will be using it and claim that amount of the cost. If the program has its own phone line, you can claim 100 percent of the cost. Of course you would claim all long-distance charges incurred by the grant-funded program.

1.2d Equipment

It is often necessary to purchase equipment in order to implement a grant program. Some funders find this expense perfectly acceptable, while others prefer you keep equipment purchases to a minimum. Remember to thoroughly justify your program's needs for and use of the equipment that you request.

If your funder allows equipment purchases, use the most accurate data you can find to budget for the price(s) of the equipment that you wish to purchase. Pay attention to the definition of equipment, which will vary by funding source. The definition will be based on cost and life span. For instance, a commonly used definition of equipment is anything with a cost of $5,000 or more per item and a life span of three to five years or more. Other grant programs may define equipment as items costing $500 or more with a life span of at least one year or more. Depending on the definition used by the funding source, items that you wish to purchase could be classified as either equipment or supplies.

1.2e Supplies

Supplies cost less per item than equipment (i.e., less than $5,000 or $500, based on the definitions of equipment in section **1.2d**) and are considered to be expendables. They can be everything from office supplies to specialized items specific to the program for which grant funding is sought. My first rule of creating grant budgets is to itemize, but in the case of supplies, particularly office supplies, detailing the cost of every pencil and paper clip is *not* necessary and certainly not feasible. Simply stating "Office supplies: $1,500" will suffice.

1.2f Contractual

Contractual covers personnel or labor costs you incur when you hire outside individuals (i.e., people who are not key project personnel) to do a specific task for the project. Paying for the services of an external evaluator, a consultant to hold a workshop, or a freelancer to design and maintain a web page for a project would all fall under the contractual category.

1.2g Construction

The name of this budget category is self-explanatory. Few grants will award funds for bricks-and-mortar construction or renovation. For those that do, the construction category in your budget is a place to detail the costs of construction and renovation activities allowable under the rules of the grant. Federal construction grants have their own budget page designed specifically for that purpose.

1.2h Other

This category is for all items that do not fall within one of the previously mentioned categories. For example, if you are proposing an educational or training program, and as part of the program you will offer scholarships to students, the "other" category could include the funding for scholarships.

If you plan to hold a workshop or conference as part of your project, the costs associated with putting on the workshop (i.e., room rental, food, etc.) could be included here. Remember to itemize these costs in your budget and use actual prices as much as possible.

1.2i Training stipends/participant support

These two budget categories are not standard categories for all grants, but I wanted to mention them because they are common in federal grants. Training stipends are often used in US Department of Education grant programs, and the participant support category frequently appears in National Science Foundation grants. When applying for grants from either of these two agencies, you will see one of these categories on the agency's budget form, and the application instructions will tell you how to use them.

1.2j Direct costs

The term "direct costs" is most often used in federal grant programs. It appears sometimes on state and local grants, but is rarely used in foundation and corporate grant programs. Direct costs consist of all the budget categories mentioned in this section and can be defined as all expenses specifically incurred to achieve the goals of a grant project or activity. These expenses can *only* be used to support that specific grant-funded program. They cannot be used for regular organizational costs.

1.2k Indirect costs

Indirect costs are defined as those expenses that support common, ongoing activities within an organization. These costs tend to be hidden in the organization's general operating budget. They cannot easily be identified and assigned to a specific budget category of a grant application and are borne by the organization whether it receives a grant or not. Like direct costs, the indirect costs category is used universally in the federal grants world, appears much less frequently in state and local grants, and is almost nonexistent in the foundation and corporate grants arena. Indirect costs are often called *administrative costs* or *overhead*. (See section **5.1** for more on the subject of indirect costs.)

2. MATCHING BUDGET

The matching budget is the part of the overall proposal budget where you reveal other sources of funding available to contribute to the project, to "match" the funding you are requesting from the grant-making organization. It is common for agencies and foundations at all levels to require that applicants provide a match in order to receive grant funds. Federal agencies will often request that the applicant organization match a specific percentage of the total cost of a project. There are two kinds of matching funds — cash and in-kind.

2.1 Cash Match

A cash match is exactly what it sounds like. Your organization has real money to contribute to the cost of the project. Instead of paying for the entire project from grant funds, the cash match is used to offset some of the project's costs.

2.2 In-kind Match

An in-kind match refers to resources contributed to a grant-funded project that are not cash. For example, personnel costs are often supported through the use of an in-kind match. Individuals may donate a portion of their time to work on a particular project instead of being paid with grant funds. Say, for instance, American Youth Agency receives a grant to provide daycare services to low-income families in the community. The grant program is under the direction of the agency's director of community outreach, who is paid by the organization, not with grant funds. The director of community outreach earns $50,000 per year and will devote 20 percent of her time over the next year to administering the grant. The in-kind benefit is calculated as follows:

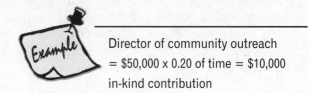

Director of community outreach
= $50,000 x 0.20 of time = $10,000
in-kind contribution

In-kind matches not only include personnel time devoted toward a project, but also cover the value of goods and services donated. In-kind costs must be quantified and may include travel, supplies, equipment, contractual services, etc.

2.3 Calculating the Match

Just as with the grant-funded portion of the budget, you must quantify and itemize the matching funds portion of the grant and must represent each year of a multiyear grant. The match column is placed next to the grant-funded column in your budget (see Sample 15). The source of matching funds is important and should be revealed in the budget justification section of the proposal. There are some grant programs that restrict the sources of matching funds, be they cash or in-kind. For example, one of the obvious restrictions is that you cannot match federal grant funds with other federal funds. Some state grant programs will not allow grantees to match state funds with other state funds.

When faced with the prospect of contributing a match to a grant project, you need to determine how much of the budget the grant program is requiring that you match. Is it 10 percent, 50 percent, 100 percent? How does the funder define matching funds: Do they have to be cash or can they be in-kind? Perhaps you are allowed to use a combination of the two. To determine the amount of funding required to meet the funder's match requirement, take the following steps:

Step 1: Determine how much grant funding you need for the project. To do this, look at the grant budget that you created. Make sure that you didn't leave out any of the project's activities and that you have the most accurate figures you were able to obtain.

Step 2: Take a look at the bottom line of your grant request. Say you've determined that you need $150,000 in grant funds to run your program, and the funder requires a match of 10 percent of the total project cost. To determine the dollar amount of the required match, divide the total amount of requested grant funding by the percentage share of the project to be funded by the grant. In this case, you divide the total amount by 90 percent because the match requirement is 10 percent.

$150,000 ÷ 0.90 = $166,667

This gives you the total cost of the project (which includes grant funds and matching funds).

Step 3: Now, to obtain the dollar amount of the match requirement, subtract the amount of grant funds you plan on requesting from the total cost of the project.

$166,667 − $150,000 = $16,667

In this example, the applicant organization must come up with $16,667 in matching funds.

Here's another example:

Step 1: The grant budget that you have created calls for $150,000 in grant funding. The federal program that you are applying to requires a 50 percent match.

$150,000 ÷ 0.50 = $300,000
$300,000 − $150,000 = $150,000

This means that you must match the total project budget with $150,000.

Step 2: When you take a closer look at the application instructions, you see that although the match requirement of the grant program is 50 percent of total project costs, only 50 percent of the match must be in cash; the other 50 percent can be in-kind. This is a great relief to your organization because it would be impossible to come up with $150,000 in cash! Now you are looking at:

$150,000 x 0.50 = $75,000

This means that for this program, $75,000 of your program's match must be in cash and the other

$75,000 can be met with in-kind donations.

You may wonder why you would inflate the budget instead of just calculating the relevant percentage of your estimated costs. In other words, in the first example, why not have the organization make up 10 percent ($15,000) of the $150,000 budget? The reason is that calculating a match this way would reduce the amount of funds you receive. Organizations tend to be cash poor, which means they are unable to invest in a new program. It's easier for them to come up with in-kind matches. Once you determine what your costs will be, the amount of grant funding is your bottom line — you want the grant to supply the needed cash, or as much of it as possible, while your organization matches this with personnel or equipment that it is going to be paying for anyway. Many organizations will pass on grants that require a significant cash match because they know they cannot meet it.

Note that if you apply for a grant that requires a cash match, you must have the money to meet this requirement. Don't try to replace it with an in-kind match.

Many grant seekers wonder where the match comes from. Here are a few possible sources for a cash match:

- General operating funds
- Fees and memberships
- Program revenue
- Other grants (make sure that the source is appropriate and allowable under program guidelines)
- Fundraising

Here are some possible sources of in-kind matches:

- Personnel time, including benefits
- Equipment
- Office space (obtain the calculation from your organization's business or finance office)
- Supplies

One final word on matching funds: Some funding agencies will allow organizations that cannot meet the designated match requirement to forfeit a portion or all of the indirect costs recoverable by the organization as a contribution toward the match. It is usually considered an in-kind match. In all my years working with and writing grants, I have never done this, but I have seen it done by others. I will explain more about indirect costs in section **5.1**, but it is enough to say here that indirect costs are overhead costs that your organization can recover for operating a grant-funded program. In my opinion it is not the best source of matching funds.

If your organization cannot meet a match requirement for a grant, I believe it is not in your best interest to "give away" costs that your organization could recover just so that you can have the opportunity to operate that grant program. This is only my opinion, but you should consider it carefully. If you decide to go ahead and forfeit some or all of your indirect costs, you should only do so as a last resort — after discussing it with your organization's executive director or business official, and *with the funder's permission*.

3. BUDGET JUSTIFICATION/ NARRATIVE

The budget justification or budget narrative accompanies the budget. This is the section I referred to previously when I said that you must "justify" the numbers in your budget. It is where you briefly explain the "why" of each line item — why the expense is necessary — as well as how you arrived at your calculation of its cost. What you want to do is show your funder the math. A vague or unjustified budget can cost you the grant if the funder thinks your numbers are unreasonable. See Sample 15 for an example of a budget and justification.

 Itemize all costs in your budget. Do not use vague terms for line items, such as "contingencies," and then assign large sums to them.

4. OFFICE OF MANAGEMENT AND BUDGET (OMB) CIRCULARS

The US Office of Management and Budget (OMB) has a special place within the executive branch of the federal government. The main purpose of OMB is to help the US Administration develop and manage the policies and programs of federal agencies. According to its website (www.whitehouse .gov/omb), "OMB oversees and coordinates the Administration's procurement, financial management, information, and regulatory policies. In each of these areas, OMB's role is to help improve administrative management, to develop better performance measures and coordinating mechanisms, and to reduce any unnecessary burdens on the public."

In accordance with its mission, OMB publishes a host of circulars that act as financial and administrative guides for federal agencies and organizations that do business with the federal government. There are six OMB circulars that will be of interest to readers of this book:

- OMB Circular A-87, "Cost Principles for State, Local, and Indian Tribal Governments"

- OMB Circular A-21, "Cost Principles for Educational Institutions"

- OMB Circular A-122, "Cost Principles for Non-Profit Organizations"

- OMB Circular A-102, "Grants and Cooperative Agreements with State and Local Governments"

- OMB Circular A-110, "Uniform Administrative Requirements for Grants and Other Agreements with Institutions of Higher Education, Hospitals and Other Non-Profit Organizations"

- OMB Circular A-133, "Audits of States, Local Governments, and Non-Profit Organizations"

The first three circulars (A-87, A-21, and A-122) deal with federal cost principles. They set out the principles and standards for determining allowable costs, both direct and indirect, of federal grant and other awards for the respective organizations covered by each circular. Their main objective is to establish consistency. The next two (A-102 and A-110) deal with federal administrative requirements, and the last one (A-133) addresses federal audit requirements. You can download them from www.whitehouse.gov/omb/grants/grants _circulars.html.

The OMB circulars reflect the structures of the organizations for which they were written, as well as the various accounting systems used by these organizations. They were created to establish uniform guidelines for the management of federally funded programs, treatment of costs, and auditing procedures.

BUDGET AND JUSTIFICATION FOR GRANT PROPOSAL

**Program Budget for the
Downtown Arts Project at the
City Arts Center**

Item	Grant Funds	Matching Funds Cash	Matching Funds In-kind
Personnel Salaries			
Project director	$30,000	0	0
Arts coordinator	15,000	0	0
Administrative assistant	0	0	5,000
Personnel Benefits			
Project director	7,500	0	0
Arts coordinator	0	0	0
Administrative assistant	0	0	1,250
Total Personnel	**$52,500**	**0**	**$6,250**
Travel	2,000	0	2,000
Equipment	1,500	0	7,000
Supplies	6,000	$4,000	0
Direct Costs	**$62,000**	**$4,000**	**$15,250**
Indirect costs	4,840	0	0
Total Project Budget	**$66,840**	**$4,000**	**$15,250**

**Budget Justification for
the Downtown Arts Project at
the City Arts Center**

Personnel Salaries

- *Project Director:* $30,000 per year grant-funded based on organization's salary schedule for regular full-time employees

- *Arts Coordinator:* $15,000 per year grant-funded based on organization's salary schedule for regular part-time employees

- *Administrative Assistant:* $5,000 per year in-kind based on current full-time position @ $25,000 per year x 20% of time donated to grant project = $5,000

Personnel Benefits

- *Project Director:* $7,500 per year grant-funded based on organization's current benefits package @ 25% of salary for regular full-time employees ($30,000 x 25% = $7,500)

- *Arts Coordinator:* $0 based on organization's current policy of not providing benefits for part-time employees

- *Administrative Assistant:* $1,250 per year in-kind based on current full-time benefits package @ 25% of salary, with 20% of time donated to project ($25,000 x 25% = $6,250 x 20% = $1,250)

Travel: $2,000 grant-funded based on local travel to promote program estimated at 5,000 miles per year x $0.40 per mile; $2,000 in-kind based on use of organization-owned vans to travel locally to bring K-12 students to performances and arts shows held downtown, estimated at 5,000 miles per year x $0.40 per mile. Total travel = $4,000

Equipment: $750 grant-funded cost to lease a copy machine for one year to support grant activities; $750 grant-funded cost to purchase a color printer to support computer-generated art projects of K-12 students; $7,000 in-kind for the value of office furniture for project staff, three networked computers with software, and two black-and-white printers used in the art classroom. Total equipment = $8,500

Supplies: $6,000 to purchase paper, canvases, paints, fabric for performance costumes, other supplies to support grant activities; $4,000 cash donated from general operating budget of organization to purchase performance and art supplies. Total supplies = $10,000

Total Direct Costs: = $62,000 grant-funded + $4,000 cash match + $15,250 in-kind match = $81,250

Indirect Costs: Based on rate of 8% of Modified Total Direct Costs = $60,500 x 8% = $4,840 ($62,000 Direct Costs – $1,500 Equipment = $60,500 Modified Total Direct Costs)

Total Project Budget: $66,840 grant funded + $4,000 cash match + $15,250 in-kind match = $86,090

Having the circulars simplifies the process of administering federal grant programs and provides consistent guidelines for applicants.

5. OTHER BUDGET CONSIDERATIONS

There are three other issues that may come up when you are preparing a grant proposal budget. Indirect costs are generally an issue for federal government grants, though they may be allowed on state or local government and foundation grants. You may also be encouraged to consider leveraging funding or be asked to create a sustainability plan.

5.1 Indirect Costs

I briefly discussed *indirect costs* in section **1.2k**. They are, hands down, the least understood part of the entire proposal-writing process. Indirect costs are also referred to as administrative costs, overhead, or Facilities and Administration costs or F&A (the latter term is used mostly by the federal government).

5.1a What is an indirect cost rate and who can get one?

I defined indirect costs as those expenses that support common, ongoing activities within an organization. They are basically hidden, by which I mean that you know these costs are being incurred, and you see the effects during the span of your grant project, but they are very difficult, if not impossible, to quantify. As a result, it is not easy to assign indirect costs to a specific category in a grant budget. You can think of indirect costs as all those costs that are *not* directly paid by the project.

For example, say your organization receives a grant award to run a program. The program is housed in a building owned by the organization. There is electricity in the building, and running water for use by project staff and participants, but the program does not pay a monthly electric bill or water bill from grant funds. Aha! The organization is bearing the costs, but the grant-funded program is reaping the benefits. This is a "hidden" expense not borne by the program.

Additionally, your organization's office of human resources helped the grant-funded program hire the project director and the rest of the project personnel. The human resources director calculated the salaries and benefits of project personnel, advertised the positions, organized the interview process, and spent time filling out paperwork for the new hires. The cost of all the work done by human resources to benefit the grant-funded program was not borne by the program. Instead, these expenses were borne by the organization.

Finally, the organization's finance office set up the new personnel in the payroll system, set up the project budget in the financial system, and worked with the project director to monitor the expenditure of funds throughout the life of the grant. Who pays for all this? The organization does. These costs are not assigned to the grant. These are all examples of indirect costs.

Most foundations and corporate grant programs will not pay for a grantee organization's indirect costs. Those that do usually set a maximum amount on indirects (say 5 or 10 percent) that the funder will pay.

State and local governments tend to recognize indirect costs more frequently than foundations. However, there are a number of state government programs that will not allow indirects to be taken on their grant awards, and the state and local government grant programs that do allow indirects will also usually cap the amount that can be taken.

The federal government, however, thoroughly understands indirect costs, and federal agencies universally accept that these costs are legitimately borne by a grantee organization. As a result, there is a system by which grantee organizations can request and receive the indirect costs for running a grant program. If you are a 501(c)(3) nonprofit organization, a college or university, or other eligible grant recipient, you are eligible to receive indirect costs.

5.1b Negotiating the indirect cost rate

The federal government and other grantors allow grantee institutions to claim indirect costs because they acknowledge that it costs institutions far more to run a grant program than what can be seen in terms of the direct costs that are actually charged to a grant. Many people think of indirect costs as additional revenue an institution receives (like a profit or bonus), but it is actually a mechanism of cost recovery that allows the grant recipient to recover those very real, but hidden, costs of running a grant program.

Because indirect costs are difficult to identify and keep track of, the federal government has developed a process by which agencies obtain an **indirect cost rate** that they use on federal grants as a mechanism of cost recovery. A rate is not arbitrarily assigned to an organization. Organizations must develop this rate by submitting an indirect cost rate proposal and negotiating the rate with the designated federal agency, usually the federal agency from which you receive the majority of your grants. This process can take a relatively long time, depending on the size and financial complexity of your organization, but at the end of it you will have established a reasonable rate of cost reimbursement that you will apply to all federal grant awards unless otherwise stipulated.

A word of caution: If you are as fiscally challenged as I am, you should not draft an indirect cost rate proposal. It is worse than doing your taxes. If you don't do your own income taxes (and I don't), then *do not* attempt to draft this proposal. Leave it to the professionals. This is a task better suited to your organization's business or finance office or the organization's accountant. If you don't have an in-house financial person, use the individual or agency your organization hires to conduct your annual audit.

When organizations begin developing their rate proposals, they should use their corresponding OMB circular as a guide (see section **4**). Information on developing an indirect cost rate proposal, also called a cost allocation plan, is available at these federal websites:

- US Department of Health and Human Services: http://rates.psc.gov

- US Department of Labor: www.dol.gov/oasam/programs/boc/costdetermination guide/main.htm

- US Department of Education: www.ed.gov/about/offices/list/ocfo/fipao/abouticg.html

Of course it goes without saying that your organization will need good, strong financial records to use in developing its proposal. If you feel confident to draft an indirect cost rate proposal yourself, gather your organization's financial statements and other financial data and then take the following steps:

1. Examine each department within your organization and identify all activities and all costs used to carry out the activities of each department.

2. If the organization currently has an allocation plan, identify the allocated costs to each department. If you don't have an allocation plan, there are three methods you can use to calculate your organization's allocated costs:

Direct allocation method. The direct allocation method is used by organizations that choose to charge their grant programs directly for all costs except those deemed "support services" (i.e., maintenance and utilities), meaning that costs are divided into two categories: (1) direct program services and (2) support services, also known as administrative costs.

Simplified allocation method. The simplified allocation method is used by organizations that perform one primary function and whose programs all benefit from indirect costs to approximately the same extent.

Multiple allocation base method. The multiple allocation base method is used by organizations whose programs all benefit disproportionately from indirect costs. In this methodology, costs are assigned to separate cost groupings (i.e., groupings for general and administrative expenses, and for depreciation and other facility expenses) and then divided between programs as appropriate.

These are the basic definitions of and premises behind the different methodologies. Detailed instructions for completing the calculation process for each method can be obtained from the departments of Health and Human Services, Labor, and Education websites cited previously in this section, as well as from the appropriate OMB circular for your type of organization. The Department of Health and

Human Services' Division of Cost Allocation has excellent review guides, as well as several examples of rate calculations, all available online at http://rates.psc.gov.

3. Classify each identified activity and its corresponding costs as either a direct cost or an indirect cost.

4. Subtract costs from the indirect cost category that are ineligible based on OMB guidelines, the regulations of the funding source, and/or other exclusions (which include, but are not limited to, capital expenditures and equipment).

5. Finally, to calculate the indirect cost rate, divide the total remaining indirect costs by the direct cost base selected for distribution of the indirect costs. (See section **5.1c**.) Your business office or accountant will provide advice on which method your organization should use.

There are four types of indirect cost rates that an organization can obtain:

- *Provisional rate.* When seeking a provisional rate, organizations are looking to obtain a temporary rate. It is agreed to in advance of the federal award and is based on an estimate of future costs. A provisional rate is retroactive, which means it can be adjusted at a later date after the true costs are determined.

- *Final rate.* A final rate is established once an organization's true costs have been determined. It is simply an adjustment to the provisional rate. However, underpayments may result from having a provisional rate in place, and you will only receive the difference

between the provisional and final rates if there are still funds from the federal award available. On the other hand, any overpayments resulting from the provisional rate must be returned to the federal granting agency.

- *Fixed rate.* A fixed rate is also agreed to in advance of a grant award and is based on an estimate of future costs. The difference between the estimated costs and the actual costs are carried forward to future years, but underpayments cannot be retroactively recovered.

- *Predetermined rate.* A predetermined rate is agreed to in advance and based on an estimate of future costs. It is not subject to adjustment, except under very rare and special circumstances. For all intents and purposes, a predetermined rate is a permanent rate.

Once your organization's indirect cost rate proposal is complete, you must submit it to the designated federal agency for approval. Prior to the approval process, there will be some negotiation as the agency reviews the proposal and supporting documentation. You may be contacted for clarification or to make changes. Once the negotiation and approval process is complete, your agency will be issued an indirect cost rate agreement to be signed by the approving agency and your organization. The rate agreement will include your specified rate, the base to which it should be applied, and the effective dates. Yes, the effective dates. Rate agreements do expire, and a new rate proposal must be submitted and approved on a regular basis if you want to maintain and continue to use an indirect cost rate for federal grant proposals. This will probably occur annually, corresponding to your organization's fiscal year.

Use the rate agreement consistently for all federal grant proposals unless otherwise noted by the funder. However, be aware that even though you have a negotiated indirect cost rate agreement, you still may not be able to recover the maximum allowable per your agreement. This is because the federal government also imposes maximum limits on cost recovery from time to time.

There are some agencies that do not allow indirect costs on certain programs at all. It varies from agency to agency. You may find yourself in a "take it or leave it" situation. You may have to accept less than the amount of indirects for which you are eligible because the opportunity to implement the program is too good to pass up.

At other times, the undue burden of "eating" either a portion or all of the indirect costs may force your organization to decline a grant award. Make sure that you make an informed decision by knowing exactly how much of the indirect costs your organization will be required to absorb.

5.1c Using the indirect cost rate

Now that you've survived the process of obtaining an indirect cost rate for your agency to use in its federal grant proposals, how *do* you use it? As I said, the rate agreement will include two important pieces of information:

- The organization's negotiated rate

- The base to which the rate is to be applied

The base refers to the cost base, meaning those portions of the proposal budget to which the program's indirect costs are applied, and can be one of the following, depending on what method is used:

- Direct salaries and wages, which may or may not include fringe benefits

- Modified total direct costs (MTDC) — modified because capital expenditures (such as equipment) and other unallowable costs are excluded from the calculation

So once you know the rate and the base, how do you calculate the indirect costs of each federal award? Take a look at the budget example in Sample 15 (on page 102). This shows indirect costs of $4,840 (based on a rate of 8 percent applied to the modified total direct costs). But let's say that the federal government has approved a rate of 32 percent applied to salaries and wages, *including* fringe benefits. This means that the indirect costs for a grant proposal with this budget would be calculated as:

$52,500 salaries/benefits x 0.32 indirect cost rate = $16,800 in indirect costs recoverable on this grant award

If the approved rate were 32 percent of salaries and wages, *excluding* fringe benefits, the calculation would be:

$45,000 salaries x 0.32 indirect cost rate = $14,400 in indirect costs recoverable

If the approved rate were 32 percent of the MTDC, not 8 percent as in Sample 15, the calculation would be:

$62,000 direct costs – $1,500 equipment = $60,500 MTDC base x 0.32 = $19,360 in indirect costs recoverable

In the last example, remember the MTDC is based on total direct costs minus capital expenditures and any other unallowable costs. Therefore, equipment, as a capital expenditure, is excluded from the calculation.

5.2 Leveraging Funding

Often grant-making agencies, including the federal government and foundations, encourage applicant organizations to **leverage funding**. This means the organizations use one source of funding (be it grant funding or otherwise) to obtain a grant award.

The idea behind leveraging is that grant funds are limited. There are a lot of worthy causes and a lot of well-written grant proposals, which highlight well-designed programs. One way that funders can distinguish one good proposal from another is by encouraging applicants to use a variety of funding sources to support a single grant program. The ability to leverage funding has a variety of positive effects, including these two:

- It increases the amount of money available to support program activities.

- It allows the organization to increase the number of people it serves and/or enhances the quality of program services.

It may be that your organization already obtained a grant to serve a particular population of individuals. When you apply for another grant from a different funding source to serve that same population of individuals, you can demonstrate your organization's ability to use the first source of funding to support similar activities that complement those in your current proposal. This will possibly give your proposal an edge over the competition in the proposal review process.

Leveraging funding is not necessarily the same thing as using grant funding to meet a match requirement of the funder. Remember that in section **2**, on matching funds, I warned you to be careful about the source of funding you use to meet a match requirement. In many cases, grant-making agencies will not allow organizations to use certain grant awards to match other grant awards.

Leveraging funding simply demonstrates your organization's ability to tap into more than one single source of funding to support your program's activities and maximize the services to your target population. In some grant competitions, leveraging funding will earn you extra points in the proposal review process. Even if this isn't the case, it is always a good idea to demonstrate that you can tap into different funding streams to support your cause, as one source of funding grants you access to another. If you can do this, put it into your proposal. The grant-making agency *will* make note of it, and it could mean the difference between receiving a grant award or not.

5.3 Sustainability Plan

Another very important section of your grant proposal is the **sustainability plan**. This is your response to a question that will be asked by funding organizations in one way or another, without exception: How does your organization plan to continue the program after the grant funding ends?

Funding organizations want to make sure that their money is invested in a good program, a program that is successful and that will continue to serve the community, solve problems, and meet the needs of the target population long after the funder's money is gone.

The primary purpose of grant programs is to address societal needs and solve social problems. If you've ever created a program to serve a need, particularly to address a social problem, then you understand that even with a highly effective program, the social problem isn't going to disappear in 12 months, or 24 months, or 36 months. This is why the issue of sustainability must be addressed long before the grant funding ends.

Grant funding is not meant to provide permanent support for the long-term operations of a program. Instead, grant funding is meant to offer start-up or seed funding for programs. This is limited in nature and available for a short period of time. Once the funding ends, organizations are supposed to have a plan to continue their programs. Grant-making agencies will request that applicant organizations address the issue of continuation funding for their programs up front ... in the grant proposal. Why would they invest in a program that will not be in existence after the grant period ends? Sustainability is relevant to funders, and they will take it into account when they review proposals.

It is in the best interest of your organization and its target population to consider the issue and make a feasible plan for continuation. Here are some examples of sources you can use for continuation funding:

- General operating funds
- Program revenue
- Fees
- Fundraising, including other grant programs

When faced with writing a sustainability plan, take the following steps:

- Address the issue. Don't ignore it and hope the funder won't notice.
- Be as specific as possible.
- Be realistic about where the continuation funding is likely to come from.
- Propose that the program be scaled back after the initial grant period ends. Justify it, knowing that it keeps your organization from having to replace the total amount of money right away.
- Write the grant proposal in such a way that the support from the funding agency is phased out over a period of time. This requires the organization to shoulder more of the financial responsibility of running the program in increments. Do this over the life span of the grant so that the process is gradual and the organization does not have to accept an enormous financial responsibility all at once when the grant is over.
- Continually seek out permanent sources of funding to support the program.

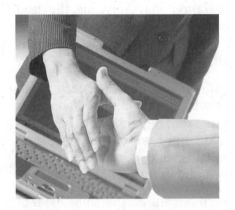

6

YOU'RE IN THE HOMESTRETCH!
THE SUBMISSION AND REVIEW PROCESSES

You're almost done. If you've reached this point, it means that all the really hard work is behind you. You've completed the research, planned your program, written your proposal, and worked out a budget. Now you need to know how the rest of the process works. In this chapter I will tell you how to submit your proposal, what happens during the review process, and a few other things you need to consider when heading into the homestretch.

1. THE SUBMISSION PROCESS

As you prepare to submit your proposal, you need to consider whether your organization will apply for a grant on its own or in a partnership; you need to ensure you are following the funder's guidelines; you need to find out if you must submit your proposal electronically; and, above all, you must be sure you meet the deadline for submission.

1.1 Applicant or Lead Organizations/ Partnerships/Fiscal Sponsorships

We saw in Chapter 2 that grant-making entities restrict which organizations can apply for

funding, but if your organization is a tax-exempt 501(c)(3) nonprofit, an educational institution, or a faith-based organization, you meet the eligibility requirements of most grant makers. If there is an interest within the organization to seek out sources of grant funding, if you have identified a good source of funding, if the organization has considered all the feasibility and planning aspects to decide whether or not to apply, if the project design is solid, and if the deadline can be met … by all means apply!

However, you also need to decide if you will apply alone or in partnership with one or more other organizations. If you decide to apply in partnership, you need to decide if you will be the lead applicant or simply a partner.

1.1a Applying on your own

In my opinion, it is often in the best interest of an eligible organization to apply for its own funding. There are several benefits to serving as the sole applicant on a grant project:

- Your organization can articulate its own vision for the program.

- You can advance your chosen method of addressing the problem.

- You can ensure that your own standards are used to spend and manage the program's funds — standards that are in compliance with all applicable laws and funder regulations and that benefit the target population of the program.

- You can build up your organization's résumé of responsible management of grant funds, which could attract more grant dollars to the organization and its programs via leveraging.

1.1b Applying in partnership

Over the past several years, the trend in grantmaking circles, from foundations to the federal government and everything in between, has been to encourage partnerships. Collaboration is seen as the key to solving social problems. One of the main reasons for this emphasis is the view that funders will achieve increased efficiency by targeting their limited resources to a "cohesive" group of organizations instead of funding one organization at a time, piecemeal.

In addition, some funders believe that requiring organizations to form partnerships in order to compete for grants will eliminate the duplication of effort in which several small organizations within a community operate several small programs serving the same population of individuals. The purpose of partnerships is to get organizations talking, exchanging information, collaborating on projects, enhancing their programs, and sharing their resources — all with the desired outcome of providing better and more efficient services to their communities.

Partnerships are great, and good partnerships are even better. In some situations, a certain organization may serve as the lead applicant; in others, it may be a partner in the grant, with another organization serving as lead applicant.

The benefits to serving as the lead applicant are similar to those mentioned above for sole applicants. Your organization has final say in the vision and form of the program, it sets the standards, and it also receives the credit for successful grant management.

My concern about partnerships is that many organizations seem to be partnering for the wrong reasons. And in other partnership arrangements, expectations are unclear. This will lead to conflict and may hinder the working relationship between the organizations in the future. Do not become one of these organizations.

If a funding agency requires that eligible applicants partner with other organizations to receive funding, and if your organization meets the eligibility requirements, it is best to seek out partners with which your organization has already developed a relationship. What's most important, though, is that your partner shares your vision of the program. The partner should bring something to the table, whether it is tangible or intangible, that will contribute to the success of the project.

 Respect your grant partners. If you are the lead applicant, give them the opportunity to provide input into the proposal *before* it is submitted to the funder. Send copies of the proposal to grant partners immediately after it is submitted to the funder; do not make them ask for it. Always keep your partners informed of the status of grant proposals. If you apply for a grant and it is not funded, let your partners know.

If your agency does not meet the eligibility requirements to apply for a particular grant, but you want to develop a partnership with another organization in order to become eligible for the grant program, my advice is the same — make sure your prospective partner shares your vision and that it brings something to the proposal. It would certainly be beneficial to partner with an organization with which you have an existing relationship.

Once you have identified a potential partner, contact the staff at that organization. Let them know about your idea for the proposal and that your organization is ineligible to apply. Invite the other organization to "participate," by becoming the lead organization. Keep in mind that the lead organization bears the brunt of program and fiscal responsibilities. If the organization's staff do not want to take on those responsibilities, allow them to decline your invitation to partner. Do not beg, coax, cajole, or do any arm-twisting to get them to agree to participate.

If they do agree to participate, make sure you work cooperatively, especially in the following areas:

- Allow the organization considerable input into the project's design.

- Determine who will write the proposal.

- Set up a schedule for proposal completion.

- Draw up a memorandum of agreement, signed by the authorizing official of each organization, that outlines explicitly the expectations and corresponding activities of all organizations participating in the project.

- Determine how funding will be administered, particularly the amount of funding each participating organization will receive in a subcontract, if subcontracts will be awarded.

Working out all the details will take some time. If there isn't adequate lead time before the proposal deadline to do so, think twice about asking at all.

Partnership arrangements can be mutually beneficial to all organizations involved if approached properly, or they can turn into a nightmare if organizations do not handle the process with respect and consideration for their partners' wishes, abilities, and limitations. Above all, do not create a hastily thrown together, ill-advised partnership arrangement just to get grant funding. It's not worth the potential problems.

 Bring grant partners into your project early in the process.

1.1c Applying with a fiscal sponsor

Fiscal sponsorships occur when an organization that applies for grant funding uses another organization to serve as its agent for the receipt and management of grant funds. This happens most often in cases in which the applicant organization has not completed its IRS "advanced ruling period," which is a sort of probationary period prior to an organization's receipt of its 501(c)(3) nonprofit status. If your organization is in this position, make sure that you select a well-established

501(c)(3) organization to serve as your organization's fiscal sponsor. The fiscal sponsor should have a history of success in obtaining and responsibly managing grant funding. Make sure that your organization and its fiscal agent have established a clear procedure for accessing and expending grant funds and complying with audit requirements.

 Read the instructions and follow them all the time.

1.2 Following Funder Guidelines

Once upon a time, not too long ago in the world of grant proposal submission, all grant proposals were made of paper — endless stacks of pages, with originals and copies bound together by big black binder clips, that were hand delivered to local funders and mailed to federal government agencies. (This was before the pervasive use of electronic proposal submission processes, which we'll discuss in section **1.3**.) How your proposal was presented was just as important to the success of your grant application as the proposal itself.

Funder guidelines for proposal submission are always a hot topic among proposal writers. For years, funders imposed what seemed to be arbitrary rules, and if they were not followed, your proposal would be thrown out before it was read. We've all heard horror stories from grant seekers who failed to include a required form with their proposals or who made a half-inch error with the proposal's margins and whose grants were returned without review.

What seems arbitrary to the proposal writer serves the funder by weeding out a few of the hundreds and sometimes thousands of proposals that it receives from grant seekers in

a given year. Strict rules for the presentation of proposals also serve the purpose of standardizing proposals, which really does make them easier to review objectively.

Funding guidelines that dictate the look of proposal applications exist at all levels, from the federal government to foundations. You have no choice but to find out what they are and follow them. If the grant program that you are applying to states that you must use 8½- x 11-inch white paper, printed on one side only, with one-inch margins all around the page, and a 12-point Times New Roman font, do it. If the application instructions tell you to number each page consecutively in the bottom right-hand corner of the page, insert a blank, colored sheet of paper between sections of the proposal, and double-space all text, do it. If you don't follow instructions, you've lost before you even begin.

 Complete your proposal ahead of time and have one or more individuals look at it before it is submitted. Often, someone with a fresh pair of eyes, who hasn't been working on the project for the past weeks or months, will be able to provide useful suggestions and may catch errors that you miss in your own editing process.

1.3 Electronic Proposal Submission

In recent years, an overwhelming number of grant makers have decided to revolutionize their grant-making processes through the use of technology. Many of them have gone digital and, using Internet-based software, have created an online proposal writing and submission process for grant applicants. I have used small, relatively simple systems belonging to local foundations. I have used larger, more sophisticated, and still fairly user-friendly systems belonging to state government agencies. I have also used several systems belonging to federal government agencies, including the king of them all, Grants.gov.

Many foundations and state and local governments have started using electronic proposal submission systems over the last several years, but many still require applicants to submit paper copies of their proposals. There is a great deal of software available to funders, particularly foundations, but it can be expensive for them. I imagine the jury is still out on whether it's worth the financial investment, especially for smaller funders.

As more funders encourage applicants to use electronic programs to submit grant proposals, the issue of who within the organization will be allowed to use the system and how the quality and integrity of the institutional grants process will be maintained become more important. This is an organizational decision, but your organization's choices should be informed by what you learned in Chapter 3. Keep the following three points in mind:

- Quality control
- Accountability
- Institutional approval

The best electronic systems for proposal preparation and submission possess features that allow organizations to manage and coordinate their institutions' grant submissions by limiting user access and requiring a higher level of institutional authority to submit proposals.

1.3a FastLane

Federal agencies have taken the lead when it comes to streamlining their grants practices and simplifying the process for funding agencies and applicants alike. I was first introduced to one of the federal government's grants management systems in fall 2001, when OCCC was writing a grant proposal to the National Science Foundation. It required us to submit through FastLane, the NSF's Internet-based grants management system at www.fastlane.nsf.gov.

FastLane supports the entire grants process from proposal creation and submission through the review process to the award phase. FastLane is even able to support the reporting requirements, program and budget changes, and financial management of funded programs. It is, without a doubt, the best grants management system I have ever had the opportunity to use. Over the years, the system has been modified, the bugs have been worked out, and its capabilities enhanced.

One of the best things about FastLane is that it is designed with the organizational grants process in mind. It allows grantee organizations to designate a single contact person who is responsible for controlling access to the FastLane system by assigning passwords to organization staff who will prepare proposals. It also allows the organization's authorized representative to review the proposal before submission and to electronically "sign" the proposal.

1.3b Grants.gov

The king of the Internet-based grant-making systems is Grants.gov. Started in the fall of 2004, Grants.gov is the clearinghouse for all federal grant programs. Grant seekers can use it to search federal grant programs (described in section **1.1d** of Chapter 2), as well as to develop and apply for grants.

As I stated in Chapter 2, Grants.gov is an excellent research tool. What makes Grants.gov unique is that it is not a single-agency based system. It is designed to support all federal agencies' grant programs — that's why I call it the king! Over the last few years, Grants.gov has modified some of its procedures and introduce enhanced functions and new capabilities. The system keeps improving.

Electronic proposal submission is the way of the future, and it may help us finally enter the paperless society, or at least the virtually paperless society, where grants are concerned.

1.4 Meeting Proposal Deadlines

Whether you're submitting electronically or the old-fashioned way, you still need to meet the proposal deadline. I could talk about deadlines ad nauseam. Grant writing is a deadline-driven business. One of the ten commandments of grant writing should be, "Thou shalt not wait until the last minute to plan, develop, write, or submit your grant proposals."

Meeting deadlines is about planning. It's no different with grants than it is in any other field. Look back on everything we've discussed in this book. It's about the process. When you know that a grant competition is coming up, make a point of refreshing your memory about everything that it's going to take to get that proposal into the funder's hands *on time*. The number one question is — when is the proposal due? Other important questions: Does the funder request a 10-page proposal or a 75-page proposal? Do you have to mail a hard copy of the proposal to the funder or will it be submitted electronically? What else will you have to do?

 You've probably heard this before, but it's good to be reminded: Grant writing is two-thirds planning, one-third writing.

1.4a Determining the deadline

Foundations establish their giving priorities and state that they will accept proposals quarterly, biannually, or annually. State and local government agencies issue RFPs in advance of a proposal's due date. The federal government announces its open grant competitions through the *Federal Register*, through Grants.gov, and on agency websites. Federal grant programs hold grant competitions on a cyclical basis — annually, every two years, every four years — whatever the cycle may be. Some federal grant programs are created due to the politics of a new administration and don't last; others may change over time. Still others, hundreds of programs, have been around a while, some for 30 years or more.

My point is that if you do the research and pay attention, you will know what's out there and what's coming — why would you ever miss a deadline or put off writing a proposal until the last minute, increasing the chance that you will write a substandard proposal and risk losing the grant award?

The federal government is notorious for the short time frame it allows between the day an RFP is issued and the deadline for proposals. Because of this you should begin planning, and even do some of the writing, for federal proposals before the RFP issue date. Use the proposal package from previous grant competitions as a guide until the new RFP is issued. Sometimes you may have to admit it's just not feasible to submit this year — in which case, plan to submit in the next round of the competition.

1.4b Meeting the deadline

Once you know the deadline, then it's time to get organized, establish a process, make a calendar, plan your activities, and set up a schedule to complete each task on the way to developing and submitting your proposal. One of the greatest compliments I have received in my career occurred while working at OCCC when a dean came into my office waving the Grant Registration and Approval Form (see Worksheet 4) and said, "There's a reason why you have us fill out that form, isn't there? It really helped me to plan out my grant project because it got me to thinking about it." My response: "Hallelujah! Somebody actually gets it!" This occurred about six weeks before the deadline of the proposal he was working on. He used those six weeks to plan, develop, write, and edit his proposal. As a result, his $100,000 grant program was funded.

 Before beginning to write each new proposal, make a checklist of all the information you need to complete the application package. Make a timeline for proposal completion. Use it throughout the writing process.

1.4c Delivering the proposal

If the proposal is to be hand delivered by a certain date and time to a local funder, do not leave your office, grant in hand at 5:03 p.m. to drive across town to drop off a proposal that is due by 5:30 p.m. You probably won't make it.

The weather may be bad. An accident on the highway may slow you down. And when you show up at 5:36 p.m., the funder will reject your proposal.

Plan ahead. When I hand deliver proposals around town, I always plan my deliveries at least four hours prior to the cutoff time. If the proposal is due by 5:30 p.m., my proposal is submitted no later than 1:30 p.m., if not a day or two earlier. Also, please note that running up and banging on the door before the office closes for the day, begging the secretary to accept your proposal that's only six minutes late, makes you look bad to funders, especially foundations. Just don't do it!

For proposals that need to be mailed, funders will give you one of two dates: a postmarked-by date, or a date and time by which a proposal must be received by the funding source. **Note:** You can't mail your application on the day that it's due. No matter where it's going, it won't make it there in time. So not only must the grant proposal be written, but the package containing the original and all requested copies of the proposal must be complete and ready to mail at least two business days in advance.

If you are mailing several days to a week in advance, regular first-class mail should be fine. The closer you are to the deadline, whether you are trying to meet a postmark deadline or a received-by deadline, the better it is to pay the extra money to have the US Postal Service or another courier ship the package overnight with a guaranteed date and time of delivery. You will receive a receipt containing the postmarked date to serve as proof that the proposal was mailed on a particular day.

For electronic submissions, organizations must register to obtain access to the electronic submission system, and this often-complex process may take anywhere from a few business days to four weeks. And gathering and entering the required information can take days. Grants.gov warns applicants that the registration process takes one to three days, but in my experience you can add another few days to that estimate. Once you are registered, you must learn how to navigate and use the system. You can do some of this at the same time that you are working on the proposal, but, clearly, the process must be completed before the proposal's due date. My personal comfort level is to finish registering in any new system no less than two weeks prior to the due date.

With electronic proposal submission comes some uncertainty; technical difficulties may arise on your end or the funder's. If your computer crashes or the server is down and there's no Internet service, you'll miss the deadline, with no recourse except to wait until next year. Another common occurrence is that a day or two before a deadline, the Internet-based system will work more slowly than usual because everybody is logged into the system at the same time, all attempting to submit their proposals.

The bottom line is that you want to avoid these problems, so plan ahead and don't wait until the day your proposal is due to begin submitting it electronically. Try to submit three to five days before the due date.

2. THE REVIEW PROCESS

You've prepared your proposal, following all the rules. You've submitted the proposal to the funder on time. Now you wait … and you wait … and you wait. How long will it be before a funding decision will be made?

If you have applied for a foundation grant, there's a good chance that the funder's guidelines state how long it takes to review applications and to announce the names of the grant awardees. The guidelines may say something similar to the following:

> Applications must be received one month prior to the foundation's quarterly meetings, held in March, June, September, and December of each year. Grants are reviewed and presented to the board for approval at each quarterly meeting. Applicants will be notified within two weeks of award approval as to whether or not they were approved for an award.

If you submitted a proposal in January, it will be reviewed before the foundation's March board meeting, and the decision will be announced within the two weeks following the board meeting. That's three months in all. I know this may sound like a long time, but if we compare this with some federal grants, this is quite a fast turnaround!

Foundations and state and local governments tend to review grants and announce awards much more quickly than the federal government. This is because they have fewer proposals to review and less elaborate review processes, as we will see in section **2.2**. The standard review period is probably one month on the short end and no more than six months on the long end. I've rarely waited more than three months to hear the status of a grant award from a local funder, including the state government.

Federal grant programs, on the other hand, have thorough and much more complicated review processes, as well as many more proposals. It is standard to wait anywhere from six to twelve months to hear whether or not your application has been awarded funding.

2.1 Federal Government Grants

When speaking of the federal government's review process, the words "fair" and "objective" come to mind. To its credit, the federal government has a standard method for reviewing proposals across the board using selection criteria and peer review.

2.1a Selection criteria (point value of proposal sections)

Federal agencies have established **selection criteria** for each grant program. This means they have assigned point values to each section of a proposal. The number of points assigned to each section tells the applicant which sections are more important to reviewers and lets them know how thorough they need to be and how much time they should devote to each section of a proposal. Selection criteria are regularly published in the application materials or *Federal Register* notice announcing a grant competition.

Because federal programs differ from agency to agency, the selection criteria and scoring systems used will vary, but the fair and objective process of scoring grant proposals remains the same. Sample 16 shows an example of selection criteria scores you might see in an application packet.

Both the *Federal Register* notice and the application package include lengthy discussions of what the proposal reviewers will be looking for in each section of the proposal, based on the point value accorded to the sections. The reviewers evaluate and score the proposals using the selection criteria.

 The federal government has the highest standards of fairness and objectivity in its proposal review process. Study the selection criteria for each federal proposal and use them to develop the best proposals possible.

2.1b The peer review process

In addition to using a scoring system to rank proposals, the federal government also uses a **peer review process**. Instead of having a federal program officer or other agency staff review proposals, the government brings in experts with knowledge of, or experience dealing with, the problem being addressed by the grant program.

A standard way to conduct the peer review is to have each proposal evaluated by a team consisting of three reviewers. Each reviewer will score each grant using the selection criteria. After this review process is complete, the reviewers get together to discuss how they scored each proposal and why. This usually results in scores being changed up or down. The reviewers will reach a consensus and rank the proposals based on the cumulative score, and these rankings will determine who does and does not receive funding.

The details of this process may vary from agency to agency, but the important thing is that the process reduces bias and subjectivity. However, the reviewers are still human, so some subjectivity can still manage to creep in (see also section **2.3**).

SAMPLE 16
SELECTION CRITERIA

1.	Need	24 points
2.	Objectives	8 points
3.	Plan of operation	30 points
4.	Institutional commitment	16 points
5.	Quality of personnel	9 points
6.	Budget	5 points
7.	Evaluation plan	8 points
Total maximum score for selection criteria		**100 points**

2.2 State and Local Government and Foundation Grants

State and local government grant programs often have review processes similar to those established by the federal government, though not as rigid. The more sophisticated agencies do use objective scoring systems and will send proposals out for peer review by experts in the field. Others, with less sophisticated review processes, may use a scoring system, but will have local reviewers or a group of in-house agency employees, with knowledge of the subject matter, evaluate proposals.

Review processes vary, but the government (whether it is federal, state, or local) is obligated to uphold the standards of fairness and objectivity and has a responsibility to be a good steward of public funds. It should not arbitrarily award grants, and if the system being used for state and local grant competitions is not clearly articulated to applicants, organizations are well within their rights to inquire about the review processes.

Foundations are another matter. They are at the opposite end of the scale from the federal government and have a great deal more flexibility to use both objective and subjective criteria to evaluate grant applications. Often foundations already have an established relationship with local grant applicants or may be familiar with the organizations' work in the community. This can sometimes influence a funder's decision favorably or unfavorably.

 Use your grant-seeking efforts as an opportunity to build relationships with funders, especially local funders. This will only serve to enhance your organization's efforts as the years go by.

One of the unique benefits for grant-making foundations that have local applicants is that they can conduct site visits before making funding decisions. A site visit is exactly what it sounds like — a "visit" from the program officers, other staff, and perhaps board member(s) of the foundation. If the decision makers would like to see your organization in action, observe your programs, or tour your facilities to help them make a funding decision, they will request a site visit. The federal government, on the other hand, does not have the luxury of visiting grant applicants before making a decision about funding. The cost and staff time necessary to visit hundreds of applicants for every grant program makes site visits at this stage simply impossible.

The balancing act foundations must achieve is to fund organizations whose activities fit with the vision and mission of the foundation while maintaining the integrity of the grant-making process and serving the best interests of the community. Too much subjectivity in the review process can create problems.

2.3 The Politics of Grants

Foundations are not immune to pressures from board members, unflattering publicity about the applicant organization, and the like. Exactly how much influence politics has on funding decisions has always been a subject of debate in the grants community. I have talked to people who insist that "so and so" got a big grant from "such and such" because the governor's wife sits on their board, or because Senator Porkbarrel's daughter completed her undergraduate degree there, or Mrs. Socialite's son received treatment at their facility. And there often seems to be some truth to it.

There are grant writers who always send a little extra "insurance" with every proposal they submit — insurance in the form of a well-placed letter of support or a phone call to an elected official or an endorsement by a well-known and well-connected individual in the community. Sometimes that works for them.

However, it's not my style to do this. Nor it is the style of most of the grant writers, college faculty, and nonprofit staff I know. I'm willing to wager that it isn't the style of most of the countless others I don't know who write grants for their organizations and their programs every day — in my hometown and across the country. All of us have been successful in the world of competitive grants at all levels from federal to state to local to foundation, and we've been competitive in a world where we weren't all competing on equal footing.

I recognize that sometimes politics does influence who gets grant funding, and I suspect that the problem is much more common at the state, local, and foundation level. I believe in the federal government's strict proposal review process. I've let it work for me and it has. I'm not so naive as to think that the federal process can never be manipulated, but I am not going to dwell on something I can do nothing about — and you shouldn't either. Instead of being discouraged by it, continue to write those grants. Of course, there's nothing wrong with the occasional well-placed letter in your proposals. But do not get caught up in the "it's who you know" game. Follow your organization's proposal development process and you will be successful in winning grant awards on your own merits.

 Do not worry about the politics involved in grantsmanship. If you develop a strong program and build a strong case for funding, the grant awards will come.

7

SO ... WHAT NOW?
AFTER FUNDING DECISIONS ARE MADE

Whether your proposal is successful or not, there are actions you should take once you receive the funder's decision.

1. FUNDED PROPOSALS — GRANT ADMINISTRATION AND REPORTING

Congratulations! Your program has been funded. Now you face the task of implementing it. And you thought writing the grant was the hard part!

Grant recipients have a responsibility to be good stewards of grant funds. Many project directors or principal investigators are primarily concerned with operating the program — the target population, the needs to be addressed, and the program's activities — as well they should be. However, the financial administration of grant funds is just as important, if not more so. If funds are improperly expended, whether intentionally or through ignorance, and the impropriety is brought to the attention of the funding agency, it could spell disaster for the organization's grant procurement program. At the very least, the organization will have to pay back some funds. At worst, the organization will have to pay back a lot of grant funds, it may be barred from submitting proposals to the funding agency in the future, and its reputation in the funding community and the community at large could suffer a great deal of damage.

Foundation and corporate grant programs are fairly simple to administer. However, the grantee organization must still account for its use of the funds. The larger the grant, the more monitoring must be done. Multi-year grants require more monitoring than one-time funding does. As you might expect, the most regulated of them all is the federal grant.

I advise any organization that has five or more multiyear federal grants to hire or dedicate a staff person to monitor the finances of those federal programs. Post-award financial administration of federal grants is regulated by the OMB circulars described in Chapter 5, section **4**. Here are some of the most important post-award financial administration tasks you must be sure to do:

- Determine allowable costs.

- Ensure you don't expend grant funds for unallowable costs.

- Recover the proper and allowed amount of facilities and administrative costs.

- Maintain records that document how each grant-funded employee's time is spent and how salary is distributed across funding streams (often referred to as "time-and-effort reporting of project personnel").

- Adhere to cost accounting standards.

For larger organizations, several systems — including accounting, procurement, personnel, property management, and travel — come into play to ensure that federal grant funds are being properly spent within federal guidelines. These activities may be spread out over several different offices. Make sure that everyone working in each activity is on the same page when it comes to administering federal funds.

 It's okay to share copies of funded proposals with other organizations. If you've already won a grant, what are you insecure about? In an organization with a centralized grants office, always check with the grant writer, principal investigator, or project director before sharing a copy of a funded proposal with another organization.

Checklist 1 contains an administrative checklist, indicating what basic administrative information you need to gather when you are awarded a grant. Checklist 2 is a project implementation checklist. For ongoing administration and reporting, use Checklist 3, while Checklist 4 lists what you need to do at the end of a grant program.

2. REJECTED PROPOSALS — WHAT YOU SHOULD KNOW AND DO NOW

Bad news. You received a letter from the funding organization ... your grant application was not selected to receive funding. What should you do now?

For starters, don't take it personally. Proposals are unsuccessful for a variety of reasons, many of which have nothing to do with the worthiness of your cause or the writing skill that went into your proposal. Competition is intense. Funding is limited.

The first thing that you need to do is contact the funder. Be warned, though: Many foundations prefer not to discuss the reasons a grant was not funded and will simply give you a vague, neutral, non-insightful answer. If that's the case, don't press for answers. You could do more damage than good. If the funder encourages you to apply again, wait until the next funding cycle and reapply with the same project or try a new one. (Foundations are likely to remember proposals that they've read and rejected in the past. If you are going to resubmit a proposal to fund a project that was previously rejected, be sure you alter the proposal and make some changes to the program's design that will catch the funder's attention.)

When it comes to federal proposals, the standard practice is for the federal agency to automatically send a copy of the reviewers' comments to the applicant organization. You might want to send a formal, written letter requesting copies of the comments in the event that this does not happen automatically. Study these comments closely. They list the scores you received on each section of the proposal. They also outline the reviewers' thoughts on the strengths and weaknesses of your program, which may help you understand why your proposal was not funded. They can also suggest how you might alter a program and/or proposal so it receives a better score the next time. Use the reviewers' comments to make changes, and resubmit the revised proposal during the next funding cycle.

Finally, keep files of all rejected proposals, including all supporting documentation used to put each proposal together. Revisit them from time to time. When the time is right, drag them out and begin to rework them. A few months can sometimes shed new light on an old idea.

CHECKLIST 1
BASIC ADMINISTRATIVE ISSUES

❏ Find out the exact amount to be awarded, including indirect costs. Is this the amount requested in the application? Is it more? Less?

   ❏ If more, what additional services will the organization be required to perform?

   ❏ If less, how does the organization need to adjust its programming and budget to reflect the reduction in services?

❏ Find out the names and contact information of the program officers at the funding agency who will handle program and financial issues.

❏ Find out the reporting requirements and the terms and conditions under which reports are to be submitted. How often are reports due (semiannually, annually, some other frequency)? What special requirements are there for completing reports, required forms, etc.?

❏ Find out what method of payment the funding organization will use. Will the funder send a check for the entire amount at the beginning of the grant, disburse funds in increments, or reimburse the organization after funds have been expended? What financial forms must be completed or, in the case of the federal government, what online-based system is used for cash drawdowns and how does the organization become authorized to use it?

❏ Find out when the organization can begin expending grant funds. If necessary, revise project start and end dates.

❏ Have the authorized organizational representative sign the grant agreement and any other necessary forms. Return the agreement to the funding agency and keep a copy for your files.

CHECKLIST 2
PROJECT IMPLEMENTATION

❏ Send a thank-you letter to the funding agency (if appropriate).

❏ Notify any project partners of the grant award and its terms and conditions.

❏ Publicize the award internally and externally.

❏ Contact the human resources office or appropriate official within your organization and advertise positions. Proceed with the hiring process according to your organization's internal rules and in compliance with funding agency rules.

❏ Contact the grants office or appropriate grants personnel within your organization and distribute copies of the award letter and terms and conditions of the grant award.

❏ Contact the business office or appropriate official within your organization and set up the grant account.

   ❏ Distribute copies of the award letter and financial terms to the business office.

❏ Contact the purchasing officer to order equipment and supplies.

   ❏ Maintain an inventory of all nonexpendable property and equipment purchased for the project.

❏ Set up any necessary subcontracting arrangements, consulting agreements, etc.

❏ Establish procedures and a timeline for carrying out project activities.

   ❏ Share the procedures and timeline with newly hired staff and the evaluator to communicate roles and responsibilities and coordinate activities of staff. (**Note:** It's important that you involve grant partners in this discussion as well. Get them into the process early and keep them involved throughout the life of the grant program.)

CHECKLIST 3
ONGOING PROGRAM ADMINISTRATION AND REPORTING RESPONSIBILITIES

❏ Keep in touch with the funding agency about the progress of the program, and let them know about any problems that may arise.

❏ Consult with the grants office or official within your organization about the progress of the program and any problems that may arise.

  ❏ Distribute copies of any correspondence between the project director and the funding agency.

  ❏ Keep the grants office informed of all changes in scope or activities of the grant program.

  ❏ Seek the assistance and counsel of the grants office to deal with any matters, questions, or problems arising within the program.

  ❏ Work with the grants office to complete and submit project reports.

❏ Consult with the business office within your organization about the financial status of the program.

❏ Monitor your budget diligently and review expenditures on a monthly basis.

  ❏ Consult with the business office about allowable and unallowable costs, the rate at which funding is being spent, and any other financial considerations.

  ❏ Work with the business office to make sure that a system is in place to track matching funds, both cash and in-kind.

❏ Establish a system of time and effort reporting for all grant project personnel, to track effort expended on grant projects. Salaries for those paid with grant funds should match effort. Effort should also be tracked for personnel whose time is donated in-kind to meet a match requirement.

❏ Maintain a current file of documentation on grant activities and budget expenditures for site visits and reports (see section **2.2** of Chapter 6). Funding agencies, especially federal funders, generally visit projects in the post-award phase. Make sure that you are ready, that program activities are progressing, and that all documentation is on hand for review.

CHECKLIST 4
GRANT CLOSEOUT

- ❏ Submit the final progress reports for program activities and financial expenditures.

- ❏ State that the project has ended, indicate which goals and objectives have been achieved, describe what services have been provided and to whom, and affirm that all the terms and conditions of the grant award have been met.

- ❏ Keep copies of both reports with proof of mailing.

- ❏ Obtain the rules that govern the disposal of grant-funded equipment and nonexpendable property.

  - ❏ Consult the equipment inventory and dispose of property according to funder guidelines.

- ❏ If necessary, refund unexpended funds or ask to use remaining funds for extended program activities. (This is at the discretion of the funding agency.)

- ❏ Retain records of the grant program according to the guidelines of your organization and, most importantly, according to the guidelines of the funder.

- ❏ Prepare and maintain files or other records in case of program and/or financial audit.

8

NOW LET ME TELL YOU
WHAT NOT *TO DO!*
EXAMPLES OF A GRANTS SYSTEM
OUT OF CONTROL

In this chapter, I detail 12 "case studies." They are drawn from my own experience as well as from anecdotes I've heard from colleagues, and they support the view that all organizations developing and writing grant proposals must establish rules to govern their grant-seeking efforts, regardless of the size or type of organization. The procedures an organization decides upon will, of course, vary by entity, but any set of rules must instill good planning and organizational accountability.

It's also a good idea to adhere to what could be called "a grants code of conduct" when dealing with funders, partners, and other organizations involved in your grant-seeking efforts. Grants office personnel should take the lead in training organization staff in the proper way to represent their institutions in the grants process.

---

1. *"OH, THEY WON'T MIND IF I ..."* Ignoring the Rules of the Funder

Scenario 1

A state agency, which acts as the governing body for the state's postsecondary educational institutions, issued a call for proposals. This call included a specific request that the responses incorporate at least one of three activities, in order to receive funding through this particular grant competition.

One of the college's deans not only had experience with this particular funding agency

in the past, but had won a grant through this exact grant program. However, the program had changed, and some activities that were funded in the past were no longer eligible to receive funding. This dean decided to submit a proposal incorporating a now unallowable activity anyway. Against the objections of the college's grants office, and without contacting the funder prior to submitting the proposal, the dean proceeded on the misguided theory that "They funded us for this the last time; they'll do it again this time."

Outcome

The proposal was not funded.

Lessons Learned

Regardless of past history, if a funder states that it will only fund X, Y, or Z activity, do not submit a proposal to fund Q. Funding sources establish criteria for funding for a reason. Deviating from the funding guidelines will only result in your organization's proposal being turned down.

If you have doubts about whether your proposal is within the rules, by all means contact the funding source and ask questions. Your institution's grants personnel are also there to assist you. Value their experience and expertise and defer to their good judgment.

Scenario 2

A local family foundation issued a call for proposals for a sizable grant to be paid out over a five-year period. This was not a general call for proposals, but a targeted call. The foundation issued invitations to bid to a few select institutions around the state. The call requested that organizations devise plans/programs to address a much-publicized national crisis that was affecting the state in which they lived.

The written RFP stated that the funder invited telephone inquiries (actually using the word "encourage") from personnel of applicant institutions in an effort to open up communication, engage in a dialogue about the issue, exchange ideas, and — if you read between the lines — "generally engage in a little politicking and allow you to lobby for your organization to receive funding." It was the perfect opportunity for the applicant organizations to meet the funder, make a good impression, get answers to questions that would help them prepare the grant proposal, and, at the same time, generate some positive PR.

At one invited institution, the program director who would be writing the grant and managing the grant-funded project did not consider himself a fundraiser, public relations representative, or schmoozer, and he was uncomfortable contacting the funder to discuss the proposal. He was the employee with the knowledge base and expertise in the subject matter addressed by the grant. It didn't make sense for anyone else from the organization to make the call, and the funder specifically wanted to speak to the potential director of the grant project. The program director designed a project, wrote and submitted the proposal, but never contacted the funder.

Outcome

The proposal was not funded.

Lessons Learned

All funders are different, particularly private foundations. This was a local family foundation, but one with deep pockets. It clearly cared deeply about the problem it was trying to solve, wanted to find the best programs for the funding, and went to great lengths to "screen" applicants.

When your organization is given one of only a few invitations to apply for such funding, and if it is within your capacity to run such a program, you owe it to your organization to put your best foot forward. Why wouldn't you want to contact the funder? Don't you want the opportunity to operate a program that would benefit your organization and those it serves? Don't you want the money? Grant programs are highly competitive, and to have the funder pare down your field of potential competitors is a blessing.

When so many funders, particularly foundations, frown on excessive contact with applicants, it is nice to have a funder that encourages an open dialogue, wants to know more about your organization, and will give you the opportunity to ask questions, determine the wants and needs of the funding organization, and, yes, do a little schmoozing. The bottom line: Capitalize on these types of opportunities.

2. *"OH, IT'S OKAY. JUST LET THE JANITOR SIGN IT."*
And Other Attempts to Circumvent the Internal Grants Process

Scenario 3

A humanities faculty member was preparing a grant proposal for submission to a federal agency grant program that had a $25,000 cap on awards. This particular proposal involved a great deal of travel. A group of university faculty would travel abroad for two weeks to study and would incorporate their learning into a new curriculum for their students. Then expert speakers would come in to present to this group of faculty on a variety of the subjects being studied. The problem was that the faculty member writing the grant had recruited a dozen or so faculty to participate in the project and was planning to bring in at least three expert speakers, all from other states. Oh, and did I mention that all these activities were to take place in another country?

You can probably guess that without a substantial cash match from some other source, 15 people were not going to be able to travel outside the United States, afford lodging for two weeks, travel within the country to visit museums and historic sites, receive a stipend, and pay an honorarium to three outside experts for only $25,000.

Instead of scaling back the project or finding other funds to leverage, this faculty member began to slash the budget and circumvent not just the internal grants process, but also the university's internal administrative rules and procedures in general. For example, state law governing colleges and universities establishes purchasing rules. One of these rules is that travel is coordinated through the university's purchasing office, which uses a designated travel agency for the purchase of airline tickets, lodging, etc. Because colleges and universities are state-supported, they must comply with applicable laws and procedures.

The faculty member writing this proposal wanted to purchase airline tickets from the Internet to save money. Though this is a common practice for the population at large, it was against institutional rules. Furthermore, quoting an Internet price in a grant budget being submitted to a funding agency does not give the funder a true picture of a project's cost. If this grant were approved, the university would have to make up the difference between the Internet price and the agency price when it was time to buy the airline tickets through the purchasing office and its designated travel agency.

This faculty member made changes to the budget that reflected three faculty members per hotel room, severe cuts in faculty stipends, and training sessions in hotel rooms rather than meeting rooms. Most bizarre of all, he explicitly stated in the proposal that some faculty were willing to sleep on the beach for a few nights!

Outcome

The proposal was not funded.

Lessons Learned

This is an extreme example of what can happen when you are dealing with individuals who neither understand nor respect the institutional grants process. When the faculty member discovered that the project was much too large for such a small budget, he should have scaled it back significantly. To alter the budget so it appears to the funding source that the project could be implemented for such a low dollar amount is dishonest and unethical. Such actions cause the faculty member, the project, the grant proposal, and the university itself to lose credibility, and the reputation of the institution suffers as a result. No doubt the grant reviewers easily recognized that the budget was incompatible with the scope of the project. However, if this had gotten past the reviewers and the grant had been funded, the university would have been responsible for implementing a project with inadequate funding.

All organizations soliciting grant funding need to implement checks and balances to ensure that internal, as well as external, requirements are being met. Grant budgets should be subject to internal review before a proposal is submitted, and the internal reviewers should look for genuine errors and for blatantly misleading proposals. It will save a great deal of trouble in the event the proposal is funded.

Again, grants personnel and grants processes are in place at organizations to ensure that the best possible proposals are submitted, resulting in a better chance that they will be favorably reviewed and be awarded grant funds. Trust in the expertise and knowledge of grants personnel. Allow the process to do its job — preserving the integrity of the organization and ensuring compliance with internal and external rules and procedures, as well as producing a high-quality, fundable proposal.

Scenario 4

One of the college's deans was charged with the responsibility of designing a program in response to an RFP from the state's post-secondary education agency. The design of the dean's program required the college to enter into a partnership with nine of the elementary schools in the local public school district. This particular dean sat on the RFP much too long and had to scramble to get the proposal in on time. This, of course, resulted in cutting some corners.

The dean needed the signatures of the college president and the public school superintendent, to show their support for the project, before submitting the grant. According to the college's grants process, all signatures required for grant proposals are coordinated through the grants office. And upon review of the proposal by the grants office, it became evident that the dean had not worked with anyone from the local school district to develop the project, even though the district was an integral part of the program. When grants office staff pointed this out to the dean one week before the grant was due, they recommended that the dean contact the principals from all nine elementary schools to get their agreement to the grant proposal. (As an aside, the first question the public school superintendent asked after receiving a copy of the proposal to review was, "Have the elementary school principals been contacted? Do they support the proposal?")

The dean failed to contact the principals, and in an attempt to circumvent the internal grants process he submitted the proposal directly to the president's office for his signature. Luckily, the president's secretary flagged the proposal, recognized that the requisite routing sheet from the grants office did not accompany it, and returned the proposal for proper routing and submission.

Outcome

The proposal was not funded.

Lessons Learned

This proposal was improperly developed and written without the knowledge and consent of all concerned parties. When this was discovered, the grant's author attempted to get the proposal okayed by the back door, sidestepping the grants office and seeking the president's signature directly. Fortunately, because the institution had a procedure in place, it was able to catch problem grants like this one before they were signed and submitted to the funding agency.

3. "YOU'RE MY PARTNER IN THIS; YOU JUST DON'T KNOW IT YET."
Building Healthy Relationships with Grant Partners

Scenario 5

Take another look at Scenario 4. Same example. Different angle. I focused on the fact that the dean attempted to circumvent the college's internal grants process in an effort to obtain the signature of the college president. However, I only touched upon the question of why. This particular college dean developed and wrote a proposal that required the participation of nine elementary schools to carry out the funded activities. Without their participation, the project couldn't be done. The flaw in developing the proposal was that the dean not only failed to allow the principals of the elementary schools to participate in the design of the program, which would have made for a better proposal, but he even failed to tell them that the grant was being written. What if the schools had decided they did not want to participate in the grant project? That possibility

was raised by the public school superintendent when he asked whether the elementary school principals had been informed about the grant proposal and whether they had given their consent to participate in the project.

Outcome

The proposal was not funded.

Lessons Learned

When a partnership amongst organizations is a primary feature required to carry out a project, it is, in a word, wrong to submit a proposal without the knowledge of the partners. Not only is it more than a courtesy to include the partners in the planning and development of the proposal, but it is also appropriate to give them a veto over provisions of the grant that they find questionable. Partners should be told exactly what a proposal contains, and it's even better to give them copies of the proposal to review before it is submitted to a funder.

In Scenario 4, the most basic and common sense approach was ignored. You simply do not write a partnership into a grant without the knowledge and consent of the partners. You give organizations the opportunity to decline participation in the proposal. If you write a proposal that describes a nonexistent partnership, you mislead the funder and you risk receiving the funding only to find that your "partners" do not want to participate. Again, this boils down to protecting the credibility and integrity of your organization.

In this case, even though the elementary school principals were eventually told about the grant, and all gave their consent before the proposal was submitted, the comments of two of the reviewers reflected the reality of the proposal's history. Their critiques stated that the need identified in the proposal and the benefits gained were one-sided. This was an obvious result of the grant being developed and written without input from several of the partners. Valuing the contributions of your partners creates stronger proposals and solidifies partnerships, as all parties feel that they have helped to influence the project's success. This proposal would likely have been funded if it had been developed and written with the participation of all parties involved.

4. *"THAT SOUNDS LIKE A GREAT IDEA … LET'S APPLY!"*
Making Promises You Can't or Don't Keep

Scenario 6

A few years ago, a K-12 school district was given the opportunity to partner on a federal grant with a local career technology center with a good reputation in the community. The RFP called for partnership arrangements and required that bridges be built between K-12 programs and career technology centers. The school district had worked with this career technology center in the past, and the two organizations had developed partnership agreements between their various programs. The partnership for the federal grant was a good fit, and they decided the career technology center would serve as the applicant organization and fiscal agent, while the school district would be a partner.

The career technology center personnel developing and writing the grant proposal contacted a school district employee they had worked with in the past and whose department they decided would be a good place from which to administer the district's portion of the program. This employee, a middle-level manager, immediately jumped at the chance to partner on the grant and committed the district's resources, most importantly space, which at the time was at a premium in most of the district's buildings.

As it turned out, the employee committed the district to the grant project without proper approval. When the school district administration discovered this and pointed out that the district simply could not commit the necessary space, the employee, embarrassed, did not communicate this information to the career technology center in a timely manner. By the time he did tell the center, it was too late to revise the proposal, and the center missed the deadline for submission. As a result, the relationship between the district and the career technology center was strained, and in the years since, the center has not asked the district to partner on this or any other grant.

Outcome

The proposal was not submitted.

Lessons Learned

One of the problems with an institutional grants process that supports the organic development of grant projects (the bottom-up approach, described in section **2.** of Chapter 3) is that employees will often commit to a grant opportunity before they know whether it is feasible from an institution-wide point of view. All they know is that it sounds like a good idea. That is what happened here. The district employee agreed to partner on another organization's grant with no authority to do so. Because this employee was unaware of the grant's time constraints, the process moved much too slowly. The district's administration should have been notified about the potential opportunity in a timelier manner, giving it a chance to respond to the career technology center with a firm yes or no. This didn't happen. By the time the administration was given

its chance and turned down the partnership, a great deal of time had passed. Furthermore, the school district employee did not tell the career technology center that the administration had turned down the project until it was too late. At that point there was not enough time for the career technology center to submit a proposal at all.

Had there been a process in place to handle a situation like this, and had it been followed, it would have provided some time to reevaluate the project. Perhaps the career technology center could have found another willing K-12 partner. Perhaps the district could have taken on a smaller role in the project.

In grantsmanship, when dealing with grant partners, it is a dangerous thing to make a promise that you can't or don't keep, for whatever reason. Do not commit to a project unless you have the authority to do so and until you know that your organization can fulfill all of its necessary obligations. It is important to maintain a good relationship with grant partners, current and future. Instead of being in competition with one another for the same grant dollars, two or more organizations can join together in a partnership for mutual benefit. This could have been an example of just that type of partnership, but that can only work in an environment of mutual respect between partners.

---

5. *"WHEN IS THAT DEADLINE? OH, GREAT, WE HAVE PLENTY OF TIME."*
The 11th-Hour Grant Proposal

Scenario 7

I wrote and submitted a five-year federal grant proposal for a social service agency at the last minute. A day or so after the proposal was submitted, the would-be project director

brought to my attention the fact that I had failed to include salary increases for subsequent years of employment. We didn't find that flaw earlier because we weren't able to edit the proposal one last time. I was writing up to the deadline, and the project director was also busy scrambling to complete her part of the proposal at the last minute.

Outcome

The proposal was funded. However, the federal agency would not negotiate an increased dollar amount to fund pay raises. The program is in the midst of a five-year run with flat staff salaries because the organization has not had the money to fund pay and benefit increases.

Scenario 8

A colleague at a state agency wrote and submitted a grant proposal at the last minute to yet another federal agency. The grant had to be submitted electronically and had to meet very specific formatting requirements, including limitations on the number of pages, margin sizes, font type and size, and line spacing. The grant was 80 pages long, and she did not have time to do that one last check before it was submitted. As a result of cutting and pasting within the word-processing program, two pages did not comply with the required margins, and when she converted the grant documents to PDF format for electronic submission, the final page spilled over to the next page, exceeding the maximum page limitation by four lines. Yes, four lines!

Outcome

The proposal was rejected before review due to noncompliance with application instructions.

Lessons Learned

These two scenarios probably seem to seasoned grant writers like careless mistakes. But they are two examples of what can go wrong when a proposal is rushed at the last minute to meet a deadline. Things get overlooked. And those things can affect the fundability of a grant proposal or, if the grant is awarded, can place the grant awardee in a position that is less than desirable.

Who hasn't been in this position? We all have. And with the best of intentions to develop, write, compile, and submit our grant proposals long before the deadline, we find ourselves, at the 11th hour, writing, rewriting, scrambling for letters of support, copying, collating, and racing to the post office, or wading through the complicated rules of electronic submission. Sometimes other obligations keep us from putting our grant proposals together, constantly pushing the project to the back burner in favor of more important tasks. We tell ourselves, "We'll get to it. When is that deadline? We have plenty of time." Some of us find ourselves constantly waiting on other individuals to do their part, write their section, give us that data we requested, or deliver that letter of support. Many others simply suffer from good old procrastination.

No matter what the excuse, it's a bad idea to prepare and submit a proposal at the last minute. I know what you're thinking … sometimes it can't be helped. Believe me, I know. But I also know what a well-thought-out, well-written grant proposal looks like: fundable. I have seen the hastily thrown together, slightly incoherent, last-minute efforts full of typos that create more questions instead of providing answers. I have woken up in the middle of the night, kicking myself over the quick and dirty proposal that I or my colleagues threw together, forgetting to calculate pay raises for salaries in subsequent years, or neglecting to include that map or floor plan or example evaluation tool.

I have countless examples of what happens when you pull off the 11th-hour grant proposal submission — examples of funded proposals, as well as those that did not make the cut. All contained errors. All could have been improved upon ... if we had just had a little more time.

Conclusion: Avoid the 11th-hour grant proposal. It's not worth it! Next time, get started early.

6. *"LET'S JUST APPLY FOR ALL OF THEM AND SEE WHAT HAPPENS."*
Ignoring Strategy When Submitting Grant Proposals

Scenario 9

The state's postsecondary education agency issued an RFP to fund camps for high school students at the state's colleges and universities. There was a modest cap on the amount of funding an institution could receive, and the RFP noted the total amount of money allotted for the program throughout the state, which was also a modest amount. There would clearly be more applicants than grants awarded, as there often are in competitive federal grant programs. However, one of the criteria to be used in judging proposals was the geographic distribution of potential grant awardees. This meant it was unlikely that any single institution would receive more than one grant award.

The grant competition caught the attention of the provost at one of the state's colleges. He was interested in cultivating an atmosphere of grantsmanship on campus, where none had previously existed, so he encouraged faculty on his campus to apply. Two faculty members, each very respected in his or her field, were interested. One was a seasoned grant writer and had spent several years honing his skills, was well known in the community, and had built relationships within the very agency issuing the RFP. This individual had received several federal, state, and foundation grants for his program. The other faculty member was a novice at grant writing but managed to design a strong program, put together a cohesive proposal, and had an excellent chance of receiving funding. The college approved the submission of both proposals.

Outcome

The proposal by the more experienced faculty member was chosen for award.

Lessons Learned

Scenario 9 describes a situation I heard about from a colleague at another college. It was a good situation to be in: Two strong proposals. However, strategy is a word that I want you to think about for a moment. Put yourself in the college's position, in particular that of the provost. What would you have done in this situation? You are trying to cultivate an atmosphere of grantsmanship among your faculty and staff. You have two capable faculty members with strong grant proposals, both equally fundable if not for the program's lack of funding. Armed with the knowledge that your institution will probably only receive one grant, regardless of how many proposals are submitted, do you allow both grants to compete on equal footing or do you submit only one grant? If you submit only one, which one?

This is where strategy comes into play. First of all, there is no guarantee, regardless of how good your proposal is, that you will receive funding at all. Grant competitions are just that — competitive. You have no way of knowing how other proposals in the competition will rate against yours. So common sense tells you that to increase your institution's chances of receiving even one award, you submit both proposals.

That being said, however, in a smaller competition, like the statewide program in this example, you can better assess your proposal's chances of being funded. It is likely that the institution will receive one award. In an attempt to cultivate a culture of grantsmanship on campus, when you have two worthy proposals it might be better strategy to submit the proposal by the less-well-known faculty member. Grants professionals have a theory that once you get your first grant, others are sure to follow. It's no secret that your first funder is the one taking the risk on a new principal investigator, project, or institution. But once grantees establish a track record of responsible program administration, other funders are more willing to take a chance on them. This would also inspire other faculty and staff who have been sitting on the sidelines to get in the game, contributing to the desired result of creating a culture of grantsmanship within the organization, while spreading success to other faculty in the institution. Employing strategy when applying for grant funding can seem risky, but as in many other endeavors, taking a calculated risk can pay off.

7. "DO THEY REALLY NEED THAT INFORMATION?"
Failing to Fulfill Your Obligations

Scenario 10

One of my colleagues went to work for a small youth services agency in 2000, becoming the agency's first coordinator of grants and external funding. Because the agency had always been small, there was no official grants office in 1993, when it won a major grant from the federal government that ran from 1993 to 1998. Instead, the agency had a grant writer who had worked part time and taken the lead in developing and writing the proposal that was awarded funding. Upon receipt of the award, the grant writer became the grant's full-time project director. Before the five-year period ended, however, the project director left the agency. She failed to submit the final report, as required under the terms and conditions of the grant award. The executive director of the agency was aware that the final report had not been submitted, but never followed up on it.

Outcome

In July 2003 (five years after the project ended), the agency received a letter of noncompliance from the federal government, stating that it had never received the final report for its grant. There was also the issue of a significant amount of unexpended funds left in the agency's account. The letter ended with a warning (I'm paraphrasing): "If you fail to respond within 30 days, your noncompliance will affect your eligibility for future funding within the agency." This letter was faxed to the executive director and promptly delivered to my colleague, the coordinator of grants and external funding, who by this time had worked for the agency for three years. She did not start working for the agency until two years after the grant in question ended, and she had inherited a single, flimsy file on the project.

She spent the day contacting employees of the federal agency, explaining the situation to them. Then she spoke with the executive director, whose secretary recommended digging into the agency's archived materials, which were warehoused in boxes stacked in some barren, secluded storage facility. She had to find these boxes and haul all three of them back to her office, where she sorted through a few hundred files, looking for information to put into a report on a grant program that had not existed for five years. She spent the week talking to any individuals still at the agency who had knowledge of the grant or who worked directly in the program. She was able to put together a pretty convincing final report, even if it was five years late and the agency had to be threatened by the federal government to produce it!

Lessons Learned

One of the cardinal rules of grantsmanship is to finish what you start. Failing to fulfill your obligations as the recipient of grant funding is a big no-no that will come back to haunt you.

When you apply for a grant, there is an implied, if not explicit, commitment that you will provide a service in exchange for funding. When you accept grant funding, there is a contract between the grantor agency and the grantee organization that states what you will be required to do in exchange for the money. There is always a final report. Sometimes there are annual reports, semiannual reports, and quarterly reports.

Many project directors, when faced with the tedious chore of filling out forms, producing reports, and documenting grant activities and outcomes, have asked, "Do they really need that information?" My answer was, "Does it matter to you?" You entered into the contract. If you are unwilling to do the work, do not accept the grant. Funding sources want to know that their investment was worth it. How was the money spent? How did it affect the organization, the clientele, and the community? Were your stated goals met?

Outcomes. Evaluations. Proof that the money was well spent. This is what funders are looking for. This is what belongs in a final report. This is what a grantee is ethically and often contractually bound to produce. If you do your part, it will ensure that your organization remains eligible to receive future funding and it will contribute to the good reputation of your organization.

---

8. *"THIS WOULD BE A GREAT OPPORTUNITY FOR YOUR ORGANIZATION."*
Letting an Outside Organization Talk You into Submitting a Grant Proposal

Scenario 11

An employee of a state government agency dedicated to advancing careers in scientific and medical research across the state wanted to submit a proposal to a federal agency's grant program. The problem was that the state agency did not fit the eligibility criteria for the program; it was not a postsecondary educational institution. Next thing you know, the dean of science at a local college received a call from the state agency employee, making a pitch to have the college become a partner for his grant proposal. The employee claimed he had the perfect concept, tailor-made to fit the criteria of the RFP. He was also prepared to write most of the grant, adding that he had a previous unfunded proposal to work from. The only catch was that the college had to take on the responsibility of being the applicant organization, fiscal agent, and primary partner responsible for grant activities. Oh, and the proposal had to be submitted electronically within three weeks.

The state employee was well known, well liked, and supportive of college faculty who applied for funding from the agency for which he worked. The college dean, who wanted to create an atmosphere of grantsmanship among department faculty and who felt he had been put on the spot, agreed to submit the proposal. The dean needed a faculty member to serve as Principal Investigator and work on crafting the proposal. The dean approached two faculty members about taking on the role of PI before finding a third who, after a great deal of coaxing and arm-twisting, agreed to be PI. It didn't help that this faculty member had never written a grant before.

Once the PI was in place, meetings were set up. The college's grants staff, which had to electronically submit the proposal, were called in. The concept made its way to paper. The provost was brought in to sell the project to the college's other administrators, and the proposal was approved for submission.

In the meantime, the state agency employee and faculty member PI set about hashing out the details of the concept. Working under the pressure of a short deadline, and using the previous grant proposal as a guide, the team worked on designing — or should I say redesigning — the program according to the RFP's guidelines. The reviewers' comments on the weaknesses of the original proposal were helpful. Unfortunately, the state agency employee believed these qualities (which were deemed weaknesses) made the proposal a better fit for the current funding source. However, neither the college faculty member nor the college's grants personnel agreed on that point.

More problematic than that disagreement were the less-than-favorable conditions under which the proposal was being prepared. The primary partners in the grant proposal had not fully bought into the proposal's concept. This was easy to understand because it wasn't their own concept. An outside organization was leading the process and imposing its own vision. The project was being led by an inexperienced, less-than-enthusiastic PI. The proposal was rushed through the college's grants approval process before the concept was fully developed. Finally, three weeks was not enough time to overcome so many disadvantages. It was not impossible, but certainly improbable.

During the last 48 hours before the deadline, the state agency employee handed the final draft to the PI, who went over it and made some mutually agreed upon changes to align the proposal more closely to the college's vision for the program. The day before submission, the PI released the proposal to the grants office, where staff spent all that day and half of the next preparing the proposal and submitting it electronically.

Outcome

The proposal was favorably reviewed, but not funded. The Principal Investigator, who still had reservations about the project design, was relieved. Ironically, the reviewers pointed out the same weaknesses mentioned in the previous application, which were points of contention for the faculty member and the college's grants personnel.

Scenario 12

A college faculty member came across an RFP issued by a federal government agency that was looking for organizations to form extensive statewide or regional partnerships to solve a particular problem. The agency was awarding three-year grants for up to $1 million to carry out program goals and objectives.

The college faculty member was blown away by the prospect of bringing in such a large grant. He was an experienced grant writer who had been awarded several grants from the state, the federal government, and foundations. He was well known in his field, and his work had enabled him to make connections with individuals in a number of public and private organizations all over the state. The grant was in his field, and his college would be the perfect partner. He had a vision, but because the RFP was issued approximately eight weeks prior to the deadline, and because he was a methodical, cautious person, with many commitments, he decided that it just couldn't be done. He did not have the time to devote to such a large-scale project. Maybe next year. That should have been the end of it, right?

Well, as you suspected, he couldn't let it go. This faculty member emailed a dozen of his colleagues around the state, boasting about his concept for the grant proposal and talking up the great potential he saw in this project. A well-written, carefully crafted proposal, with all the right elements, couldn't lose. Somebody should do it. Several emails flew back and forth between the various parties, all expressing their enthusiasm for the project. All agreed that it would be a great idea if someone applied, but no one stepped forward to take the lead.

About three weeks passed … silence. Then a renewed interest erupted from the various potential partners. Email after email was sent out over the next week. Finally a meeting was called. More email was exchanged to coordinate schedules and set the logistics of the meeting. Finally a date was set … two and a half weeks before the grant deadline.

In the meantime, the faculty member had been having ongoing discussions with a staffer in the college's grants office, keeping him abreast of developments and stating that he was pleased someone had finally stepped up and decided to submit a proposal. The college would be a likely partner and he asked the grants staffer to accompany him to the planning meeting.

The day of the meeting, all the important players arrived — representatives from state government, business and industry, and local philanthropic organizations. All were excited by the implications of partnering on such a large and worthwhile project. Everyone was on board. A 40-page proposal — no problem. A 50 percent match, 25 percent of that in cash — no problem. Two and a half weeks until deadline — no problem.

Finally the college faculty member said, "So who's going to write the grant? I made it perfectly clear that I don't have the time. The college cannot be the primary applicant. We have an internal approval process that takes more than two weeks."

The college's grants staffer could see it coming. "Well," someone spoke up, "you brought this to us. Here we are. The college *is* the likely applicant. *You* were the one who started this. *You* said it was a great idea." No amount of fast-talking or squirming from the grants staffer could stop the train from rolling. It also didn't help that the college faculty member caved in to the pressure.

So there the college was, put on the spot because the faculty member couldn't leave well enough alone, forced into the position of primary applicant on a large grant application without the formal consent of the college's administrators, two and a half weeks before the grant was due, with a faculty member/ Principal Investigator who had a concept, nothing on paper, and no time to write. This was a problem.

After much wrangling, one of the other organizations stepped in and offered its staff grant writer to do the actual proposal writing. They called the grant writer, who was out of town on personal business and — believe it or not — would not return for two weeks, put her on the speakerphone, and talked her into volunteering her services to write the grant proposal.

At that point, one of the representatives from a state agency stood up, walked over to the dry erase board, and began to outline the proposal based on the faculty member's vague concept, which no one else in the room completely understood because it had not yet been fully developed and certainly had not been clearly articulated. Nonetheless, the state rep outlined the proposal and compiled a list of necessary data. Assignments were handed out and everyone promised to go compile their assigned piece of the grant and email it to the grant writer. Everyone left the meeting enthusiastic about the proposal … except for the college grants office staffer, who was understandably miffed and who was going to have to submit the proposal electronically using a system that he had no prior experience with, and for the faculty member, who didn't know what had hit him.

To make a very long story a tad less long, the next two and a half weeks were spent explaining the outcome of the meeting to the college's provost so that he could take the decision to a body of his peers and fellow college administrators for approval. He was displeased with the way the project had unfolded, but felt compelled to participate in order to save face.

The proposal was written by a woman who did not work for the college, who knew nothing about the college, and who knew nothing about the program she was writing about. She was out of town, could only be contacted by email, and did not present a draft of the grant to anyone until 48 hours before it was due.

The faculty member was displeased with the way the project was progressing. He did not agree with the project design. He did not agree with the projected need. He did not agree with the budget. He was to be the PI, yet he no longer recognized his vision and did not want to stand behind the project. After several more twists and turns, the faculty member almost pulled the plug on the entire proposal, but things finally reached a satisfactory conclusion when one of the state agencies agreed to submit the grant and name one of its employees the Principal Investigator. The faculty member became a Co-Principal Investigator, limiting his responsibilities. The college would no longer be liable for the content of the proposal, would not have to live up to the expectations laid out in the proposal, and would not have to serve as fiscal agent.

Outcome

Much to the dismay of the faculty member, the proposal was funded. The three-year grant period was marred by one complication after another. The project did not live up to its expectations. Everyone involved knew that was because of the inflated numbers contained in the statement of need, as well as the overly ambitious and ultimately unattainable figures stated in the goals and objectives. These were the same issues that caused the faculty member to want to kill the project. The project was also hindered by a great deal of manipulation in the budget. At the end of the three-year period, everyone involved was more than happy to see the grant come to a close.

Lessons Learned

Scenario 11 and Scenario 12 are chock-full of lessons. This is the kind of thing that can happen when you let an outside organization talk you into submitting a grant proposal. For those of us in the business of grants, grant competitions come and go. They are constant. Some proposals are funded. Some are not. Some deadlines you are able to meet. Some you are not. You will be approached regularly by organizations that want to partner on a grant project. Some you will say yes to. Others you will turn down. Listen to common sense and know when *not* to apply and when to turn down solicitations to form grant partnerships.

When an outside organization approaches your organization about partnering on a grant, pay careful attention to what is meant by the term "partner." Know what types of organizations qualify as eligible applicants to apply for grants that you are considering. Often, "partner" does not imply playing a minor role in another organization's project.

Instead it means that your organization is expected to be the primary applicant/fiscal agent — the organization with the responsibility of carrying out project activities. You will often hear the phrase, "This would be a great opportunity for your organization." Be wary. Depending on the rules for applicant eligibility, other organizations may need your organization to partner because they cannot apply for funding without you. Under these circumstances, what they really mean is, "This would be a great opportunity for *my* organization, but we can't do it without you."

In both of these examples, letting an outside organization lead the proposal development process resulted in a loss of institutional vision. This is a common occurrence in these circumstances. Before you accept another's offer to partner on a grant, it is essential that you (and all other parties) understand the concept. Partners must agree on the project's design and its overall goals and objectives. If they do not agree, the result will be unhappy, disgruntled partners who halfheartedly support the project. If the concept of a grant is incompatible with your institution's vision, do not participate. If a project director or principal investigator has reservations about elements of a project, the entire project is compromised, as the project director or PI will not be fully committed to carrying out the activities of the project.

Furthermore, it is essential that your organization set up an institution-wide process for proposal development. There should be a standard procedure setting out who can develop projects and how they are to be developed. This applies to timelines and who within your organization has the authority to approve the development of proposals. If your organization does not have a process, establish one. If your organization has a process, follow it. Situations like the ones I've detailed can be avoided. It is common to feel pressured into partnering on a grant proposal, and this is exacerbated by organizations that approach you with very little lead time before the deadline. However, if your organization has a hard-and-fast rule concerning the amount of time required for proposal review, there will be no haggling about whether or not to do it, whether or not it can even be done. It simply should not be done.

9

THE REAL SKINNY ON FREE GOVERNMENT GRANTS!

Tens of thousands of Americans have seen the late-night infomercials and the Saturday-morning programs featuring "average Americans" who have applied for and received "*free* government grants" to pay medical bills, buy houses, and start their own businesses. This chapter is for all of you who want to know the truth about the availability of government money that you don't have to pay back.

From the time I began working full-time in the grants field, I have been contacted by a lot of people (and I mean *a lot* of people!) who want me to write grant proposals for them. When I get these phone calls, my first question isn't "Can I write this person a grant?" but (1) Who are you? (2) What do you do for a living? (3) Where do you work? and (4) What are you looking to fund with a grant?

The more people I talk to, the more varied their answers, but the more varied their answers, the more they sound the same:

- "I'm looking for a grant to start my business. It's a dress shop."

- "I'm looking for a grant to buy a car. I need better transportation to get back and forth to work."

- "I'd like to get a grant to develop this tract of land so I can build houses, luxury houses."

- "I had an accident last year on the job, and I'm looking for a grant to supplement my workers' compensation."

The first rule of the grants game is that, overwhelmingly, grants are not given to individuals. They are given to organizations. Individuals may be able to receive grant funding for educational purposes, and artists and writers often receive grants, but these are limited and for special purposes.

The second rule is that nonprofit organizations receive the bulk of grant funding in this country, not the private sector. Profit-making organizations and businesses occasionally receive grant funding, but it is usually for specialized technical and scientific types of projects. Much of this money is distributed in the form of government contracts.

These are the first things I say when I speak to these individuals, and, to my dismay, I am rarely believed. It took me a while to figure out why there was this pervasive belief that the government was giving away free money for almost any reason. Then one night I was watching late-night television and saw the commercials promoting — what else? — "free government grants to buy a house, buy a car, pay your medical bills." I was stunned. Over time I noticed that these infomercials popped up on Saturday-morning television as well. They would run for a few hours in an endless loop, and there was one company that seemed to be at the forefront of this particular practice.

When I was researching and writing this book, I sat and watched one of these infomercials and noticed that they receive heavy airplay right before the company is scheduled to hold a series of workshops in a particular city. They were coming to my city, with six workshops scheduled over one week, and I couldn't resist. I had to go and see for myself, and I decided to drag along my husband, who is executive director of a statewide professional association whose members often need government money.

We registered on the company's website and arrived, as suggested, 30 minutes early one Saturday morning. We pulled into the parking lot of the hotel where the workshop was to take place and saw a line of people spilling out the door of the hotel — a large hotel, by the way. I went to find the front of the line. It stretched from the ballroom door, wound through the hallways, into the lobby, out the door, and around the building. We got in line and waited for over an hour while the line slowly progressed into the building. A quick count of the rows and number of chairs in each row told me that in the ballroom alone there were about 500 chairs, every single one of them full. The presenter would speak in the ballroom, but the presentation was carried to the overflow crowd in smaller conference rooms and other areas via closed-circuit television. From the looks of it, there were at least another 300 to 500 people. We couldn't believe it! And they were having six of these things?

Well, the conference finally started, an hour and a half after it was scheduled to begin. The sales pitch was hard core. It was part church revival, part brainwashing session. The presenter was a bigmouth and incredibly rude. He called people "ignorant" at least 30 times. According to him, "Ignorant people don't get rich." It was like what a cult does to brainwash members: Insult them, destroy their self-esteem, and convince them they need the cult. That was the effect this guy was going for.

According to the presenter, the "free" money is hard to find, but it's plentiful. People don't get the money because "they don't know where to go and the government doesn't help them." He described the organization putting on the conference as an education and research entity. The organization "won't do it for you," he said, but it would "*instruct* you to do it."

He put his organization in the same category as grant writers and attorneys — except, he warned, "You will pay a grant writer or attorney from $50 to $100 an hour. They want their money up front and they bring you a grant in a specified amount of time." His organization, on the other hand, would provide "unlimited access to all its services, unlimited research assistance, access to a team of counselors, unlimited help via a nationwide toll-free number." It would "brainstorm with you, review and revise your paperwork, assist you in preparing a business plan, and provide a reference library." A person would receive all this "unlimited service" for a one-time flat fee of $999! Later he defined "unlimited" as *six months*. At the end of the six-month period, you could renew your "lifetime" membership for $24.95. I was amazed and appalled. But there's more!

At the end of the four-hour conference, when there was a frenzy to sign up members, and people were opening their purses and wallets, I was curious about the reference library, "free with a paid membership." According to the presenter, this reference library was a two-volume set of sources of "free government money," an index of federal programs and an index of local programs. I wanted to get my hands on those books, but I was not going to spend $999 to do so.

After a nice older woman purchased her membership and received her reference library, I walked over to her and asked her what she thought. She was a retired school-teacher and she was very excited. She wanted to start an embroidery business. I asked her if I could thumb through her books for a few minutes. To my surprise, when I opened the index of federal programs, I realized I was looking at a copy of the *Catalog of Federal Domestic Assistance*. Then it all made sense.

Throughout the conference, the presenter referred to all forms of government funding as "grants" and did little to distinguish between the numerous sources or funding streams. When he told the story of a gentleman who was qualified to have his medical bills paid because he had a disability, the presenter was talking about a program known as Medicaid. It's a federal health program for low-income individuals. When he told the story of the elderly couple who "got a grant to renovate their

home by insulating it from the cold," the presenter was talking about the US Department of Energy's Weatherization Assistance Program. The purpose of the program is to promote energy efficiency. The federal government gives this money to states, which in turn distribute it through local organizations. The ultimate beneficiary of the program is the local citizen, who receives assistance to weatherproof his or her home — if he or she meets low-income eligibility requirements.

The presenter did not call these federal programs by name. He didn't technically misrepresent them, but he didn't tell the truth either. The "grants" that he described in order to sell his services are not grants in the same category as those discussed in this book. Instead, they are federal programs designed to assist US citizens, based on specifically defined eligibility requirements. These programs are set up to serve a purpose and are among the many types of benefits that the federal government provides. You do not need to pay $999 to find out about social and income assistance programs. Simply contact local social services agencies. They will have all the information you need. And it's *free*.

The idea that the federal government is giving away money to help people start businesses is a myth. There is no such assistance. With the exception of block grants, which are generally provided to stimulate economic recovery in an area, government money provided to business start-ups comes in the form of low-interest loans. The US Small Business Administration, through its local network of Small Business Development Centers, can help. Instead of going to the next infomercial-advertised grants conference in your city, contact one of these *legitimate* organizations and keep your $999 to invest in your business. Bottom line: There's no free lunch!

The following Checklists, Worksheets, Samples, Resource List, and Glossary are included on the CD-ROM for use on a Windows-based PC.

Checklists

Basic Administrative Issues

Project Implementation

Ongoing Program Administration and Reporting Responsibilities

Grant Closeout

Worksheets

Organizational Capacity Questionnaire

Funder Data Sheet

Grant Proposal Efficacy Assessment

Grant Registration and Approval Form

Timeline for Grant Application

Samples

Grants Office Job Descriptions

Grant Writer Job Description

Examples of Winning Grant Proposals

Resource List

Glossary